do?

be?

do?

What to teach and
How to teach people
with developmental
disabilities

Dave
Hingsburger

Diverse City Press Inc.

Diverse City Press, Inc. (La Presse Divers Cité Inc.)
BM 272, 33 des Floralies
Eastman, Québec
JOE 1P0   (514) 297-3080

Hingsburger, David J.

do? be? do?: What to Teach and How to Teach People
with Developmental Disabilities.

1.   Behaviour therapy
2.   Teaching strategy
3.   Developmental disability

ISBN 1-896230-10-5

TABLE OF CONTENTS

Dedication

This book is in memory of Guy Henderson. He knew how to do and to be. His wife and kids, his family, his friends, his co-workers and those he served miss him greatly. Rest well, Guy.

Acknowledgements

As always I am indebted to York Behaviour Management Services for giving me the opportunity to maintain direct clinical contact with people who have a developmental disability.

In recent years I have fallen into friendship with Fred and Phyllis Wilson. They know how to be elderly without being old. When I need a question answered, Phyllis answers it. When I need an example of how to keep young, Fred gives the example. They have made me welcome in their lives. Thanks.

What can I say about Marion Hamilton? She's fun, funny and a very good friend. Marion is a combination of a mother hen and a father confessor. Everyone needs a Marion in their life.

Patty Gibson edits Community Living News for BCACL and regularly gives me the opportunity to address issues of importance to me. She has both a critical ear and an open mind, an unusual and rare combination.

Preface
Feather Weight

June 2nd.

That day will stick in my mind for a very long time. That was the day I was to begin my vacation. The day before, a friend had dropped in unexpectedly. We sat on my deck, had a beer and chatted. Nicole, my friend, asked me how I was feeling. I surprised myself by saying, "Good, I feel really good." Life had been hard for a couple of years but the pressure seemed to be easing. I was looking forward to a vacation and some time spent swimming in the lake. The next morning I woke tired. This is not like me, I am a very early morning person. I felt that I was just overtired from the long lecture season. The first day of my vacation was spent in bed.

The next day I couldn't wake up. Consciousness seemed a long way away. It was horrible to wake up but not be awake. That afternoon I sat in the doctor's office expecting a lecture about working a little too hard. Instead she sent me immediately to the hospital's emergency ward. From there I went to Intensive Care. The next day the doctor arrived to tell me that I may not survive the infection that had begun in my leg, had gone to my blood and was throughout ... me. For four days I lay feverish, alternately caused by infection and introspection.

After the funeral was planned there wasn't much else to do so I thought about my life. I had realization after realization, most of which are far too personal to relate here. But once I'd finished reviewing my personal life, I noticed something. I noticed that my *to do* wish list was very short. Moreover, it wasn't at all distressing to me that I might not get to finish it. I can, I realized, live the rest of my life without ever latticing an apple pie, without ever setting stained glass or without ever making a macramé owl. Even though these are things I've always wanted *to do,* I wasn't distressed at the idea of not doing them.

But the *to be* list!! I really wanted to learn to be more loving, to be more forgiving, to be more tolerant of those whose views are different from mine. I wanted to be more giving of my personal time to those in my personal life. I wanted to be more able to communicate love and affection to my friends and family. I wanted to learn how to be me, the me that I believe God made, the me without the all the trimmings. This journey I regretted leaving.

Then I began to think about people with disabilities. I wondered about the goals that I had set for them in the thousands of teaching programmes that I have written over my life in this field. I wondered if I had spent my time working on a *to do* list with people who were desperately in need of learning how *to be.* I wondered if I had been teaching people the functional skills of doing when they desperately needed the practical skills of being. Why had I taught isolated skills to people living isolated lives?

In a shock I realized that those with significant disabilities, those who depend on us to plan for them, those who can't clearly communicate needs and wants, those whose quality of life depends on our quantity of insight, those who hope against hope that empathy will be our primary measurement tool, those folks ... I realized, spend their lives either waiting or working. Waiting for programmes to begin or working towards the programmes' end. These folks have only one life. They have only so much time.

Then it struck me. If someone we are working with is going to take six years to learn something, that effort spent over all that time should result in some significant achievement. Bed making, shoe tying and table setting are not achievements. If someone, I asked myself as I lay dying, is going to spend a lot of time learning something, shouldn't they learn something that makes a difference? If I had to choose between making a bed and making a friend, it would be an easy choice. If I had to choose between tying a shoe and tying a game, it would be an even easier choice. It's more important to set priorities than it will ever be to set a table.

For the rest of my life I will be asking myself the following questions every morning of my life ... *do? be? do?* And I hope and pray that every time I drive to work or have the privilege of serving a person with a disability I will pause and think *do? be? do?* As I move further away from my death bed I hope I remember how I need to answer.

And for those who are wondering: The angel of death has soft wings and arms strong enough to carry even me.

Chapter 1
Yet Lag

"That was way too much fun. Just way too much." Terry Haslam, a co-worker and friend, and I were driving back to the office after teaching the final session of a sex education class. There were about thirty people who came and we were on a high because we'd had a great time together as instructors and participants. It had been fun. That morning Terry and I had talked about the session and I said that I wanted to do something different. I knew all the curriculum stuff that should be done and I knew that adult educators would go nuts if I didn't do "closure exercises". But that all seemed so formal. After all, we had spent a great deal of time together talking about intimate things. As we chatted an idea formed in my head.

"Terry," I said with the tone of voice that gave her warning. "Yes, Dave?" she responded with a wary tone of voice that said "You've been thinking again, haven't you?" I told her that I would be interested to try something very different. It seemed to me at the time that we had taught a lot about relationships, biology and that "tickly feeling" but had not taught much about genders.

With women driving in from Venezuela while men eat a Mars bar (I think that's how it goes) popular culture is full of this gender barrier stuff. Would it be possible, I mused, to teach people with developmental disabilities about communicating across the gender divide? In seconds we had a plan. We would have the women sit on one side of the room, the men on the other then we would toss a coin. The winning group would get the first crack at answering the question, "What do you want in a boy/girl friend?" Then we would see what the other side of the room heard. Terry was up for it and we headed north.

The women won the toss. We threw out the question, "What do you want from a boy friend?" The women had no problem with this question. The list was long...

WE DON'T WANT THEM TO BOTHER US ABOUT HAVING SEX ALL THE TIME.

WE WANT TO BE TOUCHED AND HELD.

WE WANT TO BE TALKED TO AND TREATED NICELY.

WE WANT THEM TO SPRUCE UP WHEN THEY COME OVER RATHER THAN COMING IN WITH STINKY PITS.

THEY SHOULD TRY TO ACT LIKE THEY ARE INTERESTED IN MORE THAN JUST OUR BODIES.

Then we asked the men, "So what did the women say?" The first guy to respond said, "They don't want to get laid." Terry and I looked at each other and then tried again, "That's not quite what they said. Try again." The next guy, figuring we didn't hear the first guy said, "They don't want to have sex." It took the next ten minutes of work to get the men to hear what the women said.

Then it was the guys' turn, "What do you want in a girl friend?" The first man to speak said, "I want her to go out for a pizza and a beer with me." Terry and I had learned, this time instead of having the men come up with a list and then talk to the women, we went one at a time.

"So, women," we asked, "What do the men want?"

"THEY WANT US TO BE THEIR SLAVES."

Terry and I were on the floor!! By the time we finished we thought we had got the men and women to listen to what each other were actually saying. As we drove, we laughed and laughed saying the session would have had the same results with participants that did not have a developmental handicap. Some things in the human condition are just so universal.

I chuckled all the way home and couldn't wait to tell this little story over dinner. When I finished we were both laughing.

"You've sure come a long way from the days of shoe tying and over correction haven't you?" The question hit me out of the blue and caused a forkful of mashed spuds to pause in mid-air. (Briefly, but a pause is a pause.)

"No, I haven't," I said, "but we have."

On reflection I would have to admit that even ten years ago (and I have been doing this for way more than ten years) teaching people with developmental disabilities about gender, gender politics, gender stereotyping would have been the last thing on my mind. Sex education was "sperm, egg, and the virtue of chastity". Education at the time was a program and the goals were functional. Teaching meant toil. Learning meant struggle.

But things really have changed. We now, I believe, pretty much universally understand the difference between skill and ability. One can have all sorts of skills and not be able. One can be able and have very few skills. They aren't the same thing at all. A skill is a task that you do with your hands. An ability is a competence that comes from heart, mind, soul or personality.

Have you ever met a person who is really, really smart? Someone who actually thinks *eschew obfuscation* is riotous graffiti? Someone who is so into math that they think that $E = mc^2$ is a mathematical equation? (To us fat folks it means Eating = Mucho Calories With [2]Helpings.) Have you ever noticed that these folks are just a tad, well,

Dull?

(You know the bladder tightener types, the folks who when they head towards you at a party you suddenly have to pee.) Being smart doesn't make someone interesting, socially skillful, a dynamic conversationalist, a sought after dinner guest. In fact, I know a guy who has yet to figure out why he is always asked to play the corpse at murder mystery evenings!?! And this guy is a psychologist!

I saw a tee shirt once worn by an attractive, if faded, blond that said *Si Hoc Legere Scis Nimium Eruditionis Habes*. I asked what this meant and discovered it means, in Latin, *If you can read this you are overeducated*. I loved it so I stood there in the middle of the sidewalk copying down a teeshirt slogan from the ample chest of a blond passerby. (For those of you afflicted with gender stereotyping the blond was a guy named Barry, and he didn't just have a muscular chest, he had Tyrannosaurus Pecs.)

So, skills and education aren't what make us able. It has taken us a long time to learn this in human services. We have been so busy teaching skills that we haven't asked fundamental questions. Questions like, "Will Jade be any more able after I teach her shoe tying?" This is an important question to ask before beginning. Given the fact that we are talking about teaching something to someone who has a very serious learning handicap (which is what a develop-

9

mental disability is), it is going to take a lot longer to learn something. If they are going to invest a lot of time and energy in learning something, their lives should be different at the end of the program. If, when we ask, "Will Jack be more able after we teach him bedmaking?" We discover the answer is "No." Then, may I ask, subtly as is my way, *Why the hell would we bother to teach bedmaking?*

So then, what do we teach? Well, the question has a simple answer and a difficult answer. The simple answer is that we teach things that are life changing; we measure this by looking at changes in quality of life. The complex answer is that we aim at teaching *skills* that lead to *abilities*. The reason that this is complex is that we have to think about how the *skill* fits into an *ability*. And then, here's the hard part, figure out how important that particular ability is in the greater scheme of life. Bedmaking, for example, makes someone able to have a neat room. Friendmaking, alternately, makes someone able to have a neat life. Now which is more important?

Whoa, Whoa, now. Don't go shaking your head and say that I picked an obvious example. You won't believe how people will disagree over these issues. My mother, for example, thought that bedmaking was the key to the kingdom of heaven. (I still think that heaven is where the good guys have their beds made by the bad guys, but my grasp on theology may be a bit weak.) Part of the problem is that it is easier to take data on simple skills and harder to measure success of more complex teaching. And governments like nice uncomplicated data. It's like they care. Yeah, can you imagine some little government social worker from Saskatchewan calling the premier of the province screaming in excitement, "The statistics are now in, this month alone 1200 people with disabilities successfully made their beds three times in a row without error, support or reinforcement!!! Hallelujah and Praise Be!"

Yesterday in the newspaper in Montreal there was a report that came out of an international conference on developmental disabilities. It reported that all these psychologists and psychiatrists got together and one of the things that they discussed was some research that showed that people with developmental disabilities live a life typified by loneliness and depression caused by isolation. Well, sit me down as I reel from the insight. What's sad is that psychologists and psychiatrists just now *got it*. A piece of research that probably took years could have been done in minutes just by asking someone who works at the front line directly with people with disabilities. (God forbid they actually ask a person with a disability!!) I wished I had been at the conference so I could have yelled out, "Oh yeah, but while they sit in utter despair and heart wrenching depression, you can bet their beds are made, their shoes are tied and all the knives and forks have been appropriately sorted! We've put hours into this work. What more do these damned disabled folks want from us?"

Perhaps they want some common sense. But we're not quite there. Yet.

Chapter 2
Taking Flight from the Past

Her arms lifted in surrender.

It was the second time that I had tried an over correction program aimed at decreasing one behaviour while I used a reinforcement program aimed at increasing another. It was the second time I had failed. But this time I noticed.

Carolyn was a face slapper. (She was many other things but to us, in that day programme, she was nothing more and nothing less than the sum of her inappropriate behaviours.) That she was also lonely, isolated, without acknowledged communication strategies, and entirely lacking of any source of affection hadn't particularly struck us. And why would it? That was the state of the art in service to people with disabilities only a few short years ago. We concentrated on her disability and deficits. We have always seemed to believe that *the quality of life = the quantity of skills*. Her program was simple: when she slapped her face, we would take her arms and pump them up and down twenty times and then redirect her to more appropriate use of her hands. After a second or two of appropriate use of her hands, she would receive a bit of verbal praise.

Two months into the program when a staff approached her with the intent of punishing a face slap, something happened. Carolyn didn't wait for punishment.

She raised her arms and began to flap them wildly. Looking like the dying swan in a bizarre ballet Carolyn, calm faced, flapped and flapped and flapped. It seemed to be a physical prayer. With each flap there was hope that her arms would somehow give her flight and take her far from the day programme, the punishing staff, and me.

We talked, the staff and I, about Carolyn. Really talked. One of the staff pointed out something odd. When Carolyn was placed into time out for her aggressive behaviour, (when we program, we program) face slapping never occurred. We decided to keep records for the next several weeks. We are good at record keeping. Sure enough she regularly slapped her face when interacting with the staff, when expectations were placed on her, when provided with "alternate stimulating activities". But never, not once while in time out.

I found this confusing. She was engaging in the face slapping, I had assumed, because she wanted attention. But in time out, she never hurt herself. In a sickening rush of understanding, I realized that Carolyn only hurt herself when we, the staff, were near her. We tried a couple of experiments. We placed her in an area where there was a selection of "alternate stimulating activities" and left her there. It took a couple of seconds for her to realize that we weren't with her. She glanced around and then slowly began to manipulate the "alternate stimulating activities" (by now you realize Alternate Stimulating Activities is politically correct newspeak for "toys" but we couldn't call them toys·

14

because the Normalization police would have descended in horror and taken them away.) When we approached her in an attempt to join in the play, she slapped herself hard across the face. It was US!! It wasn't the activities, the place, the lack of skill, the frustrations of disability, it was US!!

Who were we? Who were we, the people who caused such stress in an adult woman in a day program that our very presence caused her to inflict pain on herself? By forty-three years old Carolyn had learned that we are the people who punish, who program, who expect failure and who teach submission. Our very presence caused her anxiety.

We had to start over. We had to stop programming and start making ourselves desirable people to be around. Richard Foxx once said in a training session, "The most important thing you need to do when you start working with someone is to establish yourself as one big reinforcer." He was right. We had to change her perception of us and of service delivery. We had to desensitize her to US.

It took a lot of work. We slowly paired staff with pleasant activities. We completely withdrew all formal programming and added fun activities into her day. Then, without warning, it stopped. One day Carolyn just stopped hitting herself. Then, slowly and gently we started to teach her things that would make her life better. We started by teaching her to point to a picture that when pressed made a funny sound that Carolyn thought was hysterical. We didn't push her. We let her laugh and laugh and laugh some more and then we let her push it again. What was she learning? She was learning that to point at something would get her something she liked. Then we added other pictures and Carolyn figured out that she could talk to us through images. The ability: *Communication*. The Skill: *Pointing*. The Process: *Starting Over, Undoing the Damage, Making Up For Who We Were By Becoming Who She Needed Us To Be.*

The idea that many people with disabilities have difficulty learning due to a history of experiencing staff as highly punitive and completely undesirable people, can be difficult to see. Carolyn used one strategy, she hurt herself. Others use different strategies, some spend all their time seeking staff out and hanging around them and are constantly "attention seeking." Having mammoth egos we always see this as their desire TO BE with us wonderful people, rather than sometimes as a STRATEGY OF APPEASEMENT and an ATTEMPT AT DIVERSION.

I now believe now that if we are going to teach we have to begin first by ensuring that we are desirable people to be around. More importantly we need to be people who do not instil fear, of punishment or failure, into a person with a disability.

You know this for yourself. Have you ever tried so hard to impress someone you admire? Did you end up by flubbing entirely? Did you say or do something completely stupid? Have you ever excused yourself from the dining room table and taken yourself into the bathroom? Once there, have you ever looked in the mirror and said to yourself, "You are just a stupid nincompoop, your mother should be fined for giving birth to someone so butt ugly. Think about it fat boy the leash law was written just for you!!" (Oops, memory crept in there.)

I'm betting you have had this experience too. People you find intimidating or threatening cause you to absolutely lose skills, lose confidence, lose self respect, lose any shred of personal dignity. Isn't it awful to even think that you may have this effect on someone you work with? Someone who already struggles on a day to day basis because they are coping with a difficult disability.

When in Vancouver, I did a consultation with the Mennonite Central Committee Supportive Care Services. They were serving a number of folks who had come out of the institution. One was causing considerable distress. He was engaging in a number of self injurious behaviours. Not only that he was diving between staffs' legs and holding them tight. He was in obvious distress. We noted that in the file from the institution that he had been tied to institution beds for most of his life and his contact with staff and with the real world had been minimal.

Not really knowing what to do we started by discussing what he liked. The list wasn't long. And it sure wasn't appropriate. He liked loud noises. He liked causing loud noises. He had come up with some interesting ways to cause loud noises. That was it. Staff could think of nothing else that he truly liked.

We decided to create a box full of things that he might want to play with. The staff went shopping and found things that either made noise or felt nice. Then we set about scheduling times that the staff would approach him with the box and help him select something. At first he would take the item and pitch it hard against the floor. This wasn't reinforcing for the staff who felt that they were upsetting him with the box. I would have suggested stopping the activity, but in discussions with Lisa (the group home manager) and Christina (the behaviour consultant) it was mentioned that George had never learned how to play. To us he may look like he is throwing away an unwanted object. To him he may be "playing" in the only way he knew how. And being honest, he was successful at making the noises he liked so much.

We steadied the course and continued. Then we noticed less self injury, fewer staff attacks but most importantly a growing ease between George and the staff. He was learning how to just BE with them. They too were learning how to BE with him. And while the data points made everyone happy, what made the difference was George's growing comfort with us, with his home and with the life he now gets a chance to live.

But there is more that needs to be done. Unfortunately, people with disabilities have learned to fear more than just us and our approach. They have often also learned to fear the entire process of learning. Remember this little ditty?

No More Teachers
No More Books
No More Teachers' Dirty Looks

Many people with disabilities come out of the school system with the idea that they are the exceptional dummies who belong in special classrooms. Don't kid yourself. They hear what the other kids in their classes say. They hear the words Retard, Dummy, Idiot. Kids with developmental disabilities have trouble learning but they aren't stupid. They know that they aren't learning as well or as quickly as other students.

Some have actually come to believe that they can't learn. Some have tried to mask their fear of being dis-covered as a "non-learner" behind explosive and angry behaviours. I have spoken with hundreds of teachers who tell me of students with learning disabilities who would rather be thought of as aggressive than be discovered as "stupid".

By the time they are adults, the image they have of themselves as competent learners is destroyed. What they don't know, because it's our little secret, is that they haven't learned because we haven't learned how to best teach them.

When I was taking "Introduction to Teaching Exceptional Children", at the University of Victoria, I had a wonderful professor by the name of Dr. Geoff Hett. He was a real personal guy with a solid set of values. In one of the tests I made a *joke* about teaching a profoundly developmentally handicapped guy to compute 28 x 30 + 6. (I still have the exam, I keep it to occasionally read the note he had written in the margin of the examination booklet.) There beside my little joke was written, "An adequate teacher knows what goals to set for their students. A good teacher never ever suggests that there is something unteachable because that assumes an incompetence in the learner rather than inadequacy in the teacher. An excellent teacher would never joke about the struggles others have in learning. I think you should strive for excellence."

So the two biggest blocks to a person with a disability learning are:

Anxiety provoked by staff.

Anxiety provoked by learning.

The causes of the anxiety are many but I think the two most prevalent are:

A history of staff as superior, powerful, controlling beings.

A history of failed attempts to learn.

Getting ready to teach
(the editor's red pencil suggested this as the chapter title YAWN)

It is not over simplification to say that many people with disabilities have been in places where the atmosphere has been one of failure and defeat, where staff automatically run programmes written by others with more power in their agencies, where shoe tying has been on the goal plan for twenty years.

My radical plan?

1)   Throw out the tired old plans. Get ready to begin again. And I mean throw them out. Stop. Take a breath. Wait a bit. Gain trust. Start over.

2)   Develop a style that makes you fun to be around. Loosen up, Lighten up, Laugh it up.

3)   Don't attempt to teach until you believe that the individual has become comfortable with your presence and confident in their ability to learn.

4)   Deny denial. Don't get into a snit thinking, "Well, they have nothing to fear about me!" or "Why, I just started in the field, this doesn't apply to me." It doesn't matter that you *didn't do it*, it matters only that *it was done*. So start off by establishing yourself as a fun and pleasant human being.

21

5)   Choose to teach abilities that make a difference.

6)   Make sure that during your teaching you both laugh at least twice.

7)   If you sense a growing frustration while teaching, stop. It doesn't matter that you aren't done. Believe me you are finished anyway if you push too hard.

8)   Success should be rewarded. And success must occur every time you teach.

9)   Realize that every time you teach your main goal is to instil confidence.

10)   Strive for excellence.

Chapter 3
Bird Brains, Ships at Sea & Roo Poo

Vern Quinsey is an amazing guy. He consulted to Behaviour Management Services for a number of years and continues in his role as friend to the agency and consultant when needed. The thing that really impressed me about Vern was his adaptability to situations. He is nothing if not a clear thinker. Once over lunch I asked him what the most important fact he learned from psychology. He surprised me by drawing a picture on a napkin. The picture looked kind of like this....

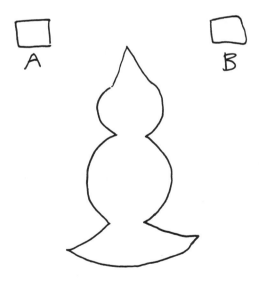

(You can tell that I wasn't ever a art major in school, huh?)

Then he told me a story about an experiment that was to test the reasoning power of birds. The researchers wanted to see if it were possible for a bird to develop a strategy. Birds were placed in a cage with two levers, named lever A and lever B. (I never made it as a researcher because I would have wanted to name them Ben and Shirl!) The cage was set up such that if the bird pecked at lever A and a food pellet came out, then it should peck again at lever A. The bird should do this until it pecks at lever A and no food pellet comes out. When this happens the bird needs to change position and peck at lever B to get the food to come out. It should then peck at lever B until no food comes out and then it should switch back to lever A. There was a very simple strategy that the bird needed to learn. In brief it was:

Win Stay - Lose Shift

Vern pointed out, voice full of irony, that the birds learned it easily. But, humans have trouble getting it.

Have you ever gone down to your car, turned the key and found the engine didn't start? What did you do? Tell the truth. Isn't the truth that you turned the key over and over again until a little key imprint was left on your finger? We tend to try over and over again things that have worked in the past. Even when they don't work anymore we just keep on keeping on.

The most important tool for teaching is the willingness to evaluate what you are doing on a moment by

24

moment basis. This means learning that if your approach goes well, is fun for the client, and learning is happening this is a *Win - Stay* position. But when frustration, anxiety and failure enters the scene this is a *Lose - Shift* position. The effectiveness of the teaching strategy is measured by its effectiveness with the client. As the British would say, "The proof is in the pudding." That's their way of saying: *Win - Stay, Lose-Shift*.

Teaching Strategies (the dull old title I was told to give this chapter, I can be difficult to work with.)

There are three main teaching strategies that can help you become an excellent teacher.

Strategy number one is simply stated: *Evaluate constantly*. Don't wait until your boss asks you to update the IPP or provide an official update for the file. Remember, it is important that the individual not sink into despair about their learning ability by facing frustration day in, day out.

Strategy number two may seem a tad controversial so let me begin by telling you a story I received over the e-mail. It has the ring of urban myth to me but I sure did laugh. I'm printing it here in exactly the way I got it...

This is the transcript of an ACTUAL radio conversation of a US naval ship with Canadian authorities off the coast of Newfoundland in October of 1995.

Americans: Please divert your course 15 degrees to the North to avoid a collision.

Canadians: Recommend you divert YOUR course 15 degrees to the South to avoid a collision.

Americans: This is the Captain of a US Navy Ship. I say again, divert YOUR course.

Canadians: No I say again ... You divert YOUR course.

Americans: THIS IS THE AIRCRAFT CARRIER USS ENTERPRISE, WE ARE A LARGE WARSHIP OF THE US NAVY, DIVERT YOUR COURSE .... NOW!!!

Canadians: This is a lighthouse. Your call.

I still smile as I type this. But beneath the humour is something quite serious. Sometimes we think that we are so big and so great that we can take on the world and move mountains. But there is the unmoveable. Disability is unmoveable, unchangeable and completely impervious to tokens, M and M's, and little bits of verbal praise.

The US naval ship represents our sense of strength, power and skill that we bring to our interactions with someone with a disability. The lighthouse represents the very real disability that ain't gonna be changed or altered as a result of our work. These two "things" keep crashing into each other.

Please don't do that, "We're all disabled" thing. It isn't true. It isn't respectful. But it is patronizing. Having a developmental disability means facing a very serious learning handicap. And it is this handicap that we must come to know, respect and even honour.

If we have the desire to teach someone who has a developmental disability we need to recognize that they will experience their disability in ways that are entirely unique to them. Two people with Down Syndrome will learn quite differently, they will process information differently, they will differ in the amount of prompting needed and they will relate to you in very different ways. The idea that there are teaching tools which will work with everyone has gone the way of the pet rock. (Cute idea, but ended up in the garage collecting dust.)

There are definite things you need to know about how a person learns. Here are a few questions that you will need to be able to answer about the learning style of a person with a developmental disability:

▸ Is Dean a visual or auditory learner?

▸ How well does Diane sequence tasks?

▸ How many instructions can Steve handle before he begins to mix them up?

▸ When interrupted can Sonia return to the task at the

the point of interruption or does she have to start over?

- How does Tim handle disruptions and distractions?

- How big or small do learning steps need to be for Tatya?

- What kind of medication is Peter taking and how do they affect his alertness by time of day?

- Is Patty a morning person or an evening person?

- What things did Keith learn easily? What is it about those things that made it easy? Was it motivation? Was it the way it was taught?

- What frustrates Kate most about learning? Is it her fear of failure? Her past attempts at learning? Or is it the approach of the instructor?

There are a million more questions, but these need to be looked at carefully. Know the person you want to teach, understand how their disability affects learning and attempt to never work "against" the disability.

A couple nights ago, I was having a beer alone in a bar in Vancouver. It was a Saturday night. Sitting nursing my beer and watching the action, time was passing slowly. Appearing from nowhere a fellow grabbed the seat next to me and said, "You want to buy some art?" Without giving me a chance to answer he pulled a piece of wood from a burlap bag. He handed me a carving he had done called, "Raven calling from wood." I took the piece and immediately fell in love with it. The wood was smooth and the lines of the carving fluid.

"That's good, you like to touch the wood," he said. I told him that I loved the sensation of wood. I then looked carefully at the raven's head. I noted that the grain of the wood over the top of the carving looked like feathers. He told me that as a carver, he had been taught by his father who was an elder from a tribe to the far north. His father told him that wood had hidden within its spirit an image that only artists could find. His job was not to create but discover. If he let the wood lead him, beauty would form itself. He needed only learn to listen to the wood and be led by its spirit to find the way of the wood.

A wise man.

The next day after church I was talking to a young guy who is taking carpentry at technical school. I asked him what happened when someone works against the grain of wood. He answered, "It scars the wood."

"Does this destroy the wood? I asked.

"No," he said but you have to work very carefully to bring its lustre and beauty back.

It's important that during our process of working with someone that they discover their own natural abilities, talents and dreams. Heather had that damn thing called potential. She lived in a twenty-four hour full support group home but really didn't need that level of support. But every time the staff tried to teach her something she would become upset and quite nasty. This frustrated the staff because they were simply trying to help her meet a personal goal. She wanted to live on her own in the community. They just wanted her to learn the skills so that her dream would become a possibility.

But, oh did she fight programming. She became quickly frustrated and no matter how much the staff tried to use reinforcement, it just didn't work. We tried motivation scheme after motivation scheme, nothing worked. Finally at a meeting one of the front line staff said, "I just don't think she gets it." I didn't understand and asked for clarification, "I don't think she understands that what we are trying to do today is aimed at getting her where she wants to be tomorrow. I think she thinks that we are all just mean for not letting her move."

What the staff was saying was that Heather's disability didn't allow her to connect items in a sequence and therefore couldn't be goal-driven. Heather, like other people with disabilities have to be able to understand a basic equation in order to really use reinforcement well. That equation? If $A = B$ and $B = C$, then $A = C$. This is simple but requires a certain degree of abstraction that some folks with disabilities, like Heather, aren't able to do easily.

When I came back the next week to the group home they had come up with a wonderful plan. They had made a bristol board suitcase and pasted it on her wall. Every task that Heather had to learn was represented by a picture and pasted around the suitcase. Heather was told that when she learned a skill it would be packed into her suitcase and when the suitcase was full, she'd move.

It worked.

You see reinforcement is highly effective but it has to be understood. We had been working against her disability, against the grain and in opposition to the "spirit of the wood." By understanding how Heather experienced a develop-mental disability we were able to come up with a plan that made sense. To her. (It had always made sense on paper.)

Strategy number two then is...

Respect the disability. Let's recognize that no matter how much we teach and how much we program, the person will still have a developmental disability at the end of the day. Let's make peace with the disability. Our job isn't to eradicate disability, it's to give the learner strategy to live well in spite of and including their disability.

Strategy number three is quite simple, *Establish*

commonality. A friend of mine once remarked that everything came so easily to me. There were tones of frustration, envy and jealousy in his voice. This sort of surprised me because he was a cool guy with a trim waist and great teeth. I saw a card yesterday at the card shop that had a picture of an extraordinarily handsome man wearing only cutoff jeans, the caption read, *What we're looking fo*r. Inside was a picture of a balding fat guy wearing a too tight tee shirt and displaying a gut busting out of Bermuda shorts. The caption read, *What's looking for us.* He is the outside of the card, I'm the inside. I'm not used to being envied by the one of *them*.

He went on to say that everything I did came easy but in particular, the writing and the speaking. For him, he said, those things were a struggle. Well, whoa, now. Writing for me is a constant challenge, I face fear and anxiety every time I sit down to type. And speaking, I still get a sick stomach and overwrought nerves at the idea of having to get up in front of an audience. I told him, but he didn't believe me. The fact was that he had never seen or heard me in my private moments when I had a BM session. (That's Bitch and Moan!) He didn't understand that I looked at my life as being in a constant FOG (Frigging Opportunities for Growth).

People with disabilities must think much the same of us. Everything comes easy. Nothing is a problem. We have cars, money, sex when we want it. (Yeah right, we work in social services: our cars are dead before they are paid for, our salary barely buys celery, and sex whenever we want it

... not true ... but a handy idea!) As far as they are concern, we never have to deal with frustration, anger, heartache, loss, pain, overwhelming grief and confusion. (Be honest, you experience all these each time you open your pay package. Or look at yourself in a swimsuit!)

I think it's important to become a little bit more real when at work. There is nothing wrong with coming in to work after having spent two hours fighting traffic (Canadian version) dodging bullets (American version) being Bobbied (British version) or stepping in Roo poo (Australian version) and saying something like, "Whew I've got to sit me down (CA) wipe the blood off (US) pay my ticket (UK) and wipe off (AUS)." Talk through your emotion, discuss aloud potential solutions, and then demonstrate resolution. Let them see the process, let folks with disabilities realize that we all face life hassles and we all have to handle them in the best way we can. They aren't different from anyone else emotionally, they aren't alone in the realization that life smells a bit more like a fart than a flower, we all are in this together.

When I was at University I hired someone to help me understand statistics. The woman had a calculator for brains and the personality of a digital doofus. She made me feel really stupid from the moment she said in a tone of voice that dripped with sarcasm and superiority, "So just what don't you understand?" My answer, "Why I hired you." We parted company. But I was desperate for help. Over coffee one day, getting late in the term, I overheard a woman at the next table say that she had a real tough time with the Stats course but managed to struggle through to a C+. To me, a C+ represented an incredible achievement bordering on the miraculous so I approached her and asked her if she would consider tutoring me. She laughed at first, but when she figured out I was serious she agreed. She was fabulous. She explained things clearly and pointed out the areas where she had had the most difficulties and taught me how she solved her problems. I passed. I didn't live up to her shining C+, but a pass is a pass.

I could learn from someone with whom I shared struggle. She used her experiences of difficulty to enrich her teaching. She had no difficulty in presenting herself as another struggling human helping out someone else. (This isn't that *we're all disabled* stuff, this is a recognition that all humans struggle as we swim upstream.)

Chapter 4
Whips and Chains

You are your own greatest teaching tool. What you do and how you do provide a model for those you serve. It is a tremendous mistake to think that teaching happens only at scheduled teaching times. In fact, the entire time you are with people with disabilities who receive your care, you are teaching. Unfortunately, without noticing this we end up teaching things we don't want to teach.

Have you ever noticed that a lot, and I mean a lot, of people with developmental disabilities have trouble with personal space? Have you noticed that sometimes when a person with a disability wants to talk to you they stand too close, put their face right into your face and talk intently about something? Ever wonder why someone might do this? Well, look around at what happens. When staff want to talk to a person with a disability about something important we often put our hands on their shoulder, lean our faces in and talk intently. What is the individual learning?

My guess is that they are learning that when you have something important to talk about, grab, stick and talk. This is on the "unofficial" social skills curriculum of most group homes. I was asked to provide a consultation for a man with a disability charged with the assault of a female clerk in a department store. Staff were shocked because he had never engaged in this kind of behaviour before. Too, they reported that he had been in a good mood when leaving home because his parents had given him some birthday money to spend "any way he wanted."

He headed to the mall to buy himself a watch he really wanted. The store was open, the watch was there but the clerk paid him very little attention. Finally, he decided to use his *I have something important to talk about* social skills that he had learned at home. He came at her from behind, grabbed her arm, tried to put his face in hers and when she screamed, he just grabbed harder and started to yell about the watch so she would understand he just wanted to buy something. He was charged with sexual assault. He wasn't convicted but he is no longer allowed to go to the mall. A born shopper, his quality of life has been drastically reduced.

We are always teaching. So we had better be sure that what we "do" and what we "say" match up. People with disabilities, by and large, are better visual learners than they are auditory learners. This means that your "do" yells and your "say" whispers.

The Teaching Tools (the boring title the publisher wanted me to give this chapter)

There are twelve basic tools that can be used to teach. These tools need to be adapted for each person you want to teach. Remember to:

Wait make sure that you have spent some time with the person. Don't jump in and teach what you think they need, look at their lives and ask what they really need to learn. It is better to spend a little time in thought and introspection than to dive into a program that may teach a skill but make no difference. It is better to employ empathy than objectivity any day of the week. Ensure that you:

Gain trust. Some of the most important information is garnered through relationship rather than through penmanship. Who cares what someone else wrote about the person? This is now, this is you and them. Before you begin anything make sure you have put other things aside and watched how the individual you want to teach operates in the world and how they process information. Only then do you start.

Tool # 1: Task Analysis

I hate doing a task analysis. They are boring, tedious, and incredibly important all at the same time. A task analysis is, there is no other way to put this, an analysis of a task. This is where you break the task down into its component parts. Here is where it becomes important that you know the learning style of the person you serve. You need to know how big or how small the steps need to be. Doing a task analysis of every day skills is relatively easy. In fact, I'll bet you used a task analysis just recently. Do you recognize the following?

VEGETARIAN SHEPHERD'S PIE
(this is no joke, this is my favourite recipe)

Ingredients:

Potato Layer

4 large potatoes, peeled and cubed
water (save the water the potatoes are boiled in!)
1 tbsp. unsalted butter (margarine)
1/2 cup potato water or skim milk
salt to taste

Filling

10 oz. of firm tofu, frozen then thawed (24 hours in the
refrigerator or 8 hours at room temperature), then shredded
(easily done in a food processor!)
1 large onion, chopped
1/4 tsp. thyme
1/2 tsp. coriander
sprinkling of pepper
3/4 cup walnuts, minced
1 tbsp. lemon juice
2 tbsp. tamari sauce
salt

How To Put It Together

Potato Layer

1.   Cover the cubed potatoes with lightly salted water (at least 3 cups). Simmer till cooked. Drain and save the water for gravy. Mash the potatoes with the remaining potato layer ingredients.

Filling

1.   While the potatoes are cooking, sauté in a large skillet, the onions with thyme, coriander and pepper, until translucent. Stir in the walnuts and shredded tofu. When heated through, add the lemon juice, tamari sauce, and salt to taste. Remove from the heat and place in a casserole dish.

Mushroom Gravy

3/4 lb. mushrooms, sliced
3 tbsp. tamari sauce
1 1/2   cups hot potato water
2 tbsp cornstarch dissolved in 1/2 cup potato water
salt and pepper to taste

1.   Preheat the oven to 400 degrees.

2.   Sauté the mushrooms in a little potato water along with the tamari and pepper, until tender. Add 1 1/2 cups of the potato water and bring to a boil. Combine the cornstarch with the half cup of potato water and slowly add this to the skillet. Simmer over low heat, stirring often, until the gravy is thick and

smooth. Pour the gravy over the tofu mixture in the casserole and stir briefly to combine.

3.   Top the casserole with the mashed potatoes, then bake for 15-20 minutes until the top is golden. Serve immediately. Enjoy.

So a task analysis is a recipe. I bet most of you could easily write down a recipe for your favourite meal. If you can do that, then you are on your way. You will now be writing recipes about how to live!! That is so cool, huh? The recipe above is a perfect example of a great task analysis, it tells you what you need, then systematically tells you how to do it. The same thing should be true of every task analysis you do. Let's take a look at tooth brushing. We begin with the individual in the bathroom in front of the mirror. The toothpaste and tooth brush is kept in a small glass beside the sink. OK...

Step 1:   Take toothpaste from glass.
Step 2:   Remove top.
Step 3:   Take brush from glass.
Step 4:   Squeeze toothpaste on brush. (Not from the middle you nincompoop. How many times have I asked you to squeeze from the bottom? And to think I am going to have to live the rest of my life with a middle squeezer? Oh Yeah, well I'd rather be a middle squeezer than a damn old geezer.)
Step 5:   Set down toothpaste.

Step 6:   I think you get the point.

Now, what do you think, is the task analysis done above for someone who learns quickly, taking big steps? Or is it for someone who learns more slowly taking little steps? Well, in fact, it is for someone who learns quickly. The steps are huge and make a lot of assumptions. Re-read the task analysis and see how many assumptions this analysis makes of the learner.

Well, let's see, they can recognize toothpaste and distinguish the brush from the tube. They can take off a cap and set it down. They know how to squeeze gently (yeah, yeah, yeah, and from the end) and can squeeze onto a small surface. They know where to put the tube and can co-ordinate the hand movements necessary to manipulate brush and tube.

There are basically four kinds of tasks for which someone may need an analysis. Tooth brushing is a physical task. There are also social tasks, emotional tasks and artistic / spiritual tasks.

Social tasks: Many people with disabilities have difficulty with social skills. You may need to look at teaching a variety of social skills. Anything from greeting skills to abuse prevention skills. These are much more difficult to write and require a lot of assumptions about what the person can do. Looking at a greeting skill, the task analysis might look like this:

Step 1:	Distinguish person as stranger, friend, staff or family.
Step 2:	Greet appropriately by selecting from the following behaviours, waving hand, hand-shaking, saying hello or giving a hug.
Step 3:	Wait for person to respond.
Step 4:	Return to appropriate distance, if necessary.

These steps are so huge that they each may need to be broken down further.

Emotional Tasks: These involve the appropriate expression or suppression of emotions. Goals here may be things like frustration tolerance; anger management; assertion training. Even so, it's important to have an understanding of how you are going to teach this skill.

When working with someone who had difficulty with the emotions of fear and anger (who doesn't) I teach basic relaxation skills. Two women in my office had adapted the relaxation procedure and made it very simple. The decision was made to teach a relaxation procedure due to the fact that the client was seemingly unable to control his temper and moreover once he lost it, it was gone. We thought that if we could teach him what it was to be relaxed then we could start to teach him to recognize the basic body cues to identify anger, frustration and other negative emotions. The procedure used the following task analysis:

Step 1: Sit upright, butt to the back of a chair, feet flat on ground, hands resting comfortably in lap.

Step 2: Close eyes.

Step 3: Take slow deep breaths.

Step 4: Arch foot.

Step 5: Relax foot.

Step 6: Raise feet off floor.

Step 7: Set feet down gently.

Step 8: Pull in stomach.

Step 9: Relax stomach.

Step 10: Raise and tense arms.

Step 11: Lower and relax arms.

Step 12: Raise shoulders against neck.

Step 13: Lower shoulders to normal position.

Step 14:   Scrunch face.

Step 15:   Relax face.

Step 16:   Say, "I feel relaxed."

Step 17:   Breathe quietly for 4 to 5 minutes.

Step 18:   Open eyes.

This simple task analysis kept us on track and enabled us to slowly go through the procedure. Because it had been adapted for people with learning disabilities, each step was very visible. YOU GUESSED IT. The above task analysis was the 2nd one we used. The first had the client's eyes opened so that he could see what he was doing. Then we taught him to do it with his eyes closed.

Artistic or Spiritual Tasks: These are perhaps the most difficult to analyze. Everyone approaches issues of art or spirit in very different ways. Interestingly, when talking to Cindy Caprio-Orsini (author of a book on art therapy with people who have a developmental disability and who have been traumatized) told me that when setting artistic goals, one usually had to begin by "letting go" and then going from there. I think the same is true of Spiritual Goals.

The fact that these may be difficult to do doesn't mean that we shouldn't try. Check through your client's file and see how many of the goals that have been set fall into physical, social, emotional or spiritual. I bet you find tons of physical type goals with decreasing numbers down to artistic / spiritual goals. Interestingly, for us quality of life is usually calculated the other way around!

Tool # 2: Instruction Giving

Here's where you will find the fact that you did a task analysis of tremendous benefit. You will already have an understanding of the complexities of the task and therefore will more likely be clearer when you are giving instructions. The difficult issue is understanding the difference between concrete words and abstract words. Look at the sentence below, determine if it uses concrete words or abstract words:

The chair is white.

As you have guessed, this is a trick question. All words, by definition are abstract. When we are speaking, then, we may assume that since we are using simple words we are being understood.

Take a look at this other simple sentence. It would be easy to understand wouldn't it? Or would it?

You need to calm down when you are angry.

Now there are a bunch of really simple words that, when combined, mean nothing!! What does calm down mean? Does it mean taking a big breath or two? Does it mean going for a walk? What does angry mean? Does it mean yelling? Does it mean a fast heart beat and shallow breathing occurring after someone called you a name? What does it mean?

We need to learn to monitor our language to keep it simple and understandable. Try a little experiment that a professor at school had us try. Three students tried and failed, then she called on me. I had no problem with this (but I have an advantage). See the drawing below. Before turning the page attempt to describe this drawing to someone. Do it in such a way that they will be able to draw from your description. Wait! Before you begin. You can't use the words: Circle, Triangle, Square. OK, now try.

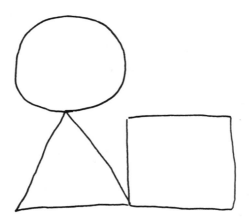

Now here's how I did it. Draw a pie. Underneath the pie draw a piece of pizza with the pointy end touching the pie. Now on the right side of the pizza, draw a piece of cake the same size as the pizza and have its lower corner touch at the bottom of the pizza slice. Using things that someone understands, one doesn't have to "understand" geometrical forms. (Fat people are naturally good at this game. I walked by the three thin little losers with a sense of complete victory. I went out that night and ate me a triangle, a circle and a square!!)

Practice your instruction giving until you can do it easily and simply. You will find that this may actually effect your view of life. Things really are much simpler than we make them out to be.

Tool # 3: Adaption

Me. Me an activities coordinator and counsellor. Me, the guy who failed physical education so badly that they had to come up with a letter below F, gets a job as an activities coordinator. Well, it was summer. I needed a job. And the department of mental health needed an activities coordinator. The job was working with kids with mental health needs (in this case that meant kids who needed a whopping dose of parental affection and approval) who were educationally falling between the cracks (which is spin doctoring for *I don't care what you do with that brat as long as he's out of my classroom*) whose behaviour was problematic (which is behaviour therapist for *won't give in without a battle*) and unresponsive to treatment (which is social services for *has given up on themselves and others*). It was a great summer. I really liked these kids. And once they got over the horrible idea of having to be seen with a big fat guy, they liked me too.

One of the last events of the summer was going off to a church camp for three days. I was really pleased with how the summer had gone. Even though nothing much was expected from me, the program or the kids. We did well. I saw that the kids really responded to expectations, boundaries and praise. They saw that I responded well to respect and learned that even fat people have feelings. I wanted them to become comfortable in their own skins and learn that they didn't have to *prove* anything to anyone because they were already OK. These kids had learned how to cope with a world that was harsh and unkind. Their strategies needed work, but they knew how to cope. I wanted them to find new defense strategies, new ways of defining themselves and learn that those who are in power aren't always right. Big lessons for a summer and I didn't fool myself, I just wanted their journies to start.

By the time camp came we were a pretty solid group. We had managed to get a couple of volunteers to join us and together it was great. At camp we did the typical camp stuff. And by the way they fed us you'd think that a hot dog with mustard, relish and onions was the distilled version of the four food groups. Which I muse, they just may be. Everything went well until Sunday.

We made our way to a wilderness chapel. It was beautiful. The pews were rough hewn logs and the pulpit was overgrown with moss and ivy. It would be a struggle to not believe in the divine when sitting in such simple beauty. The minister was some guy who clearly had been trained in youth ministry as was evidenced by his cool clothing, and his liberal use of the word *cool*. He took me aside and said that he had worked up a sermon that was aimed at helping the troubled kids. My *oh shit* warning system kicked in but I figured what damage could one sermon do?

Well did he preach. It was kiddie hellfire and damnation. I contained myself until he told a story. I don't know if the story came out of some book called, "50 ways to make kids feel guilty" but it could have. It was about this crab family. It seems that crabs walk sideways even though they know that God wants them to walk frontwards. So what these crafty crustaceans started doing was walking frontwards on Sundays. During the week they would practice at walking frontwards but mostly they gave in to their desires to walk sideways. And what they didn't realize, as sinister shellfish are sorrowfully stupid, is that God was watching them all week long. And God knew whenever they walked sideways. GOD WASN'T FOOLED BY THEIR PRETENDING TO WALK FRONTWARDS ON SUNDAY. BECAUSE GOD KNEW THAT THEY WERE NOTHING MORE THAN SIDEWAYS WALKERS. THEY

WOULD GO TO HELL FOR TRYING TO FOOL GOD ABOUT WHO THEY REALLY WERE. *GOD ONLY LOVES THOSE WHO FOLLOW THE RULES!! IF YOU BREAK THE RULES YOU ARE SCUM HEADED FOR HELL. JUST LIKE THOSE CRABS!!!!!!!!!!!!!!!!!!!!!!!!*

I lost it. These kids had rightfully come to doubt parental love. They had a right to a hope in a divine love. I knew that for myself a faith in the absolute love of God is what gets me though the day. These kids, these human sideways walkers, had a right to the same.

I interrupted him mid-condemnation and told him that his sermon missed an essential point. He was flabbergasted at my intrusion. His confusion seemed to delight all the kids, troubled or not. He asked me my point. I asked him why God would make sideways walkers and then demand that they walk frontwards. I asked him if a loving God would create something that would have to struggle against its nature, a nature that God created in the first place. I asked if maybe what God wanted was for the church to understand that sideways walkers were made to walk sideways. I suggested that every person had two jobs, the first was to determine who God made them to be and the second to struggle to be that person. The church, I said, has similar jobs. The first, was to recognize that God created a world of diversity. The second, was to honour and welcome everything that God made. Even if this meant building the occasional pew on a SLANT.

He stormed out of the chapel and in doing so, as I artfully pointed out, he had to turn sideways to slide through the brush at the entrance. A few years later I told a friend about this little act of rebellion on my part and she said, "You think that minister was bad? Let me tell you the schools are full of teachers who only want forward walkers." The trouble is that most people think there is only one way to get to a destination. Until ministers, teachers, social workers all figure out that sideways walkers can get to the same place in a different way we are going to constantly go against the grain of human abilities.

Someone who drops soap every time they pick it up is a sideways walker. Instead of trying for a thousand years to teach them to hold soap, why not buy soft soap that you just use a pump to access. For those sideways walkers who have spent a greater part of their adult life tying shoes, how about slip ons. A guy who cuts himself into teeny tiny bits every time he shaves needs to become a bearded sideways walker. Shouldn't we first adapt to who the person is and how they learn before we force them into a lifetime of frustration? Freedom from failure comes from adaptation and alteration. We'd better be careful because if we don't respect the people we serve there may be a march one day with hundreds of people following a banner saying...

Sideways Walkers Unite!!!

Tool # 4: Parallel Talk

Parallel talk is a wonderful strategy. It just simply means talking while doing. If a person with a disability is about to go on an instructional program about dish washing, then why not have them watch you do it for a couple of weeks first. Sit them down on a stool, chat about stuff and then as you do the task say out loud what you are doing. "I'm turning on the cold water first, now I'm adding the hot water. I need to wait for a second and then test the water temperature. I sure don't want to burn myself. Now that the temperature is right I'm going to put the stopper in the sink. I do that by putting it in its place and then twisting. There, I can tell it's working because the water is filling the basin. Now it's time for soap."

Describe what you are doing, during a casual time with the individual wherein there is no pressure to learn anything. There are no charts and forms. No demands or expectations. Just a chat (you should be talking about other things as well) and a few laughs (which can help take the

52

fear of failure away) while you are doing something.

Entry into teaching by allowing time for observation, for hearing how it's done in a relaxed atmosphere is a wonderful way to begin. By the time the person starts they are well ahead. And since you are going to probably use chaining anyways, it makes sense to begin at the beginning. In this case that's simply an observational stage.

You can bridge the gap between the observation with parallel talk with...

Tool # 5: Apprenticeship

By introducing the person to the task in a gradual way you may actually be able to teach without it being noticed in the slightest. By using a period of observation and parallel talk you can move gently towards the teaching program by apprenticeship.

Back at the kitchen sink now. "Would you mind getting the soap for me? I've let my hands get wet. Thanks I appreciate the help." Tee hee hee, a step is being taught in a natural, *can you help me out*, kind of way. "Oh and would you mind turning off the water? I'm over here getting some dishes. Thanks bud." This is a co-operative way of engaging the person in the task which is almost entirely non-stressful.

For those folks who are finally and blessedly off those thousand year long bed making programmes and on to learning something useful, fun and life enhancing, apprenticeship may be the answer. Using apprenticeship as partial participation without the stress of having to learn is a wonderful and respectful way of keeping the person involved without pressure. Maurice Feldman, a psychologist friend of mine, was rightfully worried that staff may read this book and see it as an excuse to run around doing housework without interacting with others. His point is well taken, we can become so involved in all there is to do, that we forget that we are also supposed to be with folks with disabilities. So drop the programme but maintain the interaction. Apprenticeship can be the goal in and of itself.

Tool # 6: Waiting

"You must be so patient." If you have been in social services more than six minutes you've heard this a thousand times. Well in fact, most of us in human services aren't particularly patient and those that are get nothing done. Patience, however, is a virtue when teaching. When a person with a developmental disability is learning it requires that they use processing skills which may be a real challenge for them. I've seen several situations where staff prompt folks with disabilities too quickly. Remember once you give a prompt, you need to WAIT for the person to hear it, process it and then act on it. For folks without a learning disability this happens fast. For those with disabilities this may take a moment. If you don't wait, you will probably issue the prompt again, and again and again. The result is a series of prompts that come too quickly. Each time the learner needs to abandon the last process, hear the new prompt and then process again. If we don't wait for the act stage we end up with folks who become entirely prompt dependant. So give the instruction and then, there's no nice way of saying this, shut up, take a breath, and wait.

(This is hard to do and even harder to remember. I wrote the above section on waiting several weeks ago. I am now sitting in a hotel in Roanoke, Virginia. It's early in the morning and I'm happily editing away. While re-reading this part of the book I got a creeping sense of guilt. On Monday of this week I did a teaching session for people with developmental disabilities. One young man who attended put up his hand volunteering to role play. When he came up, I gave him his scene. He stood there for what seemed like hours. I didn't want to either lose the flow of the workshop or to embarrass him so I gave him the question again but reducing what he had to do. Again he stood there, his teeth grinding in what I took to be anxiety. So again, I offered him a simplified version of the original request. Finally, Pat, a woman with Down Syndrome sitting near me said with frustration, "Give him a minute, it takes him time to talk. Oooops. I waited and when the words had made their tortuous journey from mind to mouth he answered quite clearly. Imagine being "outed" as an impatient and somewhat inadequate teacher in front of those very people you are supposed to have some skill in teaching. Not a great moment in Hingsburger History.)

Tool # 7: Chaining

All chaining means is linking on part of the task analysis to the other. It emphasizes teaching one skill and then moving on to another and another and another until the entire task is learned. There are two kinds of chaining, forward and backward.

Forward chaining means focusing on the first step of the analysis and then moving systematically through the skill. Backward chaining means starting at the last step and then backing up. Most physical skills are taught best using backward chaining. The social, emotional and artistic / spiritual tasks are most often best taught by laying a solid groundwork and then working through the skill.

In either case, it's best to hook the learner on the task. If you are teaching shopping, for example, take the individual shopping with no pressure to learn. Make the whole skill just plain fun. Then slowly and surely begin to teach. The very best teaching is done by introducing your teaching strategy without making a big deal about the fact that ... *YOU ARE LEARNING SOMETHING NOW* ... or **WARNING: PROGRAM IS ABOUT TO BEGIN**. No matter if you are using forward or backward chaining, the point is that the task analysis, the chaining procedure and the use of reinforcements should be done as naturally as possible. These things are for your benefit to keep you on track and help you teach.

I love using backward chaining as it allows the person such an experience of success. When teaching bed making, for example, you take the learner to their room and YOU DO ALL THE FIRST STEPS OF THE ANALYSIS. But while doing it you are using parallel talk. Remember that parallel talk means that you are describing what you are doing. You would be pulling at the sheets saying, "I'm pulling at the sheets to straighten them out." It feels silly at first but it is providing a lot of information. The learner sees the task being done, hears a description of the task, then is taught to do just the last step, pulling the comforter up. Then you go crazy with giving reinforcement for a job well done.

When that step is learned then you work on the next to last, fluffing the pillows (that was a slang term for something very vulgar when I was growing up). Then you link them together. Each step is a link in the longer chain of the skill. Remember to use reinforcement and to ensure that each skill is well learned. Voilà, backward chaining.

Tool # 8: Modelling

Modelling is a very simple procedure to do. As the word implies it is the simple demonstration of the skill for the individual. It's the big sister *here let me show you* strategy. This is where all that work that you put into becoming a powerful positive person is going to pay off. The individual, having come to respect you, like you and most importantly, not fear you, is more likely to respond to you as a model. Advertisers know this inherently; ever notice how when some model or sports guy (men who get paid millions of dollars to play with their balls aren't heroes in my humble estimation) engages in some really stupid or nasty behaviour they are dropped promptly from the endorsement circuit. People aren't likely to want to emulate someone they don't respect. The same is true here.

Remember though, you are always modelling. One of my friend's favourite stories was the night when she was entertaining her in-laws and her little five year old girl was playing quietly in the front room. The radio was on softly, she had created the perfect idyllic setting for her husband's family. All of a sudden her beautiful flaxen haired child let out with a loud curse, "Hey you, yeah you with the Baboon Ass!! You can suck my dick!!!" Her plate almost hit the floor.

It took a while but soon they learned that any time the child heard a car chase, car tires squealing or revving engines, she would cuss a blue streak. Turns out that Daddy approaches driving as a combination race track and primal scream therapy sessions. The little girl had learned to respond to certain sounds or situations with a particular kind of language.

We are always being watched by those who depend on us. Our power as models occurs most often when we aren't thinking about it. As such it can be a pretty useful tool when we do think about it. Let's say you are going to teach someone how to greet friends when they come in the door. All you need to do is ask them to watch you do it and then have them try themselves. You can run through something two or three times, using the "first watch me," and "now you try" approach.

I know this is kind of an aside, but once I was on a plane and had gotten bump up fare to first class. I was joined by a woman who was put together with a combination of parts from an adolescent male's wet dream and a bucket of beauty products. I swear as she walked you could hear the wind whisper behind her one word over and over, "liposuction, liposuction, liposuction." She acknowledged me with the disdain that some people who feel that they personally created their fast metabolism sometimes do. Like God was their assistant at the mixing of the gene pool!! Can't you imagine God as a counter boy at "Cheekbones Я Us!?!" Well, I'm sure she could.

I asked her what she did for a living. "Model," came the one word, but a breathy word it was, response. "Humm," I mused. "And you," she asked with incredible boredom. "Well, I have two jobs. I teach and I model too." The teach part didn't surprise her but the model part shocked her. "What do you model?" "Social skills and artful conversation," said I quickly and brightly. "And what do you teach?" "Well amongst other things I teach masturbation skills?" Thus ended our conversation.

Well she asked!!!

And I did tell the truth.

Tool # 9: Prompts

Prompting comes naturally. In fact, often I have to fight the *prompting urge*. Have you ever stood in line at one of the bank machines (you know those things the bank created so you wouldn't have to stand in line inside the bank where it's comfortable and warm rather than outside in the snow, sleet and drizzle) behind someone who just doesn't quite know how to use the machine? You see them pause, read the instructions, tentatively put their card in the machine, stop, read the instructions again, then they punch in their PIN, read the instructions again. And all the while you are standing behind them feeling moss grow up the north side of your body. Don't you almost have to tie your hands at your side so that you don't start prompting them? Don't you want to say things like, "You push this button and then that button then put in the amount you want and then, the most important part, after the money comes out you get the hell out of my way?"

There are three kinds of prompts, verbal, gestural and physical prompts. Many people place these in some kind of hierarchical order thinking that the use of one, like verbal, means that the person is better at the task than if it was necessary to use another kind of prompt, like physical. To me, this is a meaningless activity, a prompt means that assistance was necessary for the completion of the task. Dithering over what kind of prompt was used really doesn't make any difference.

60

When I worked direct care in the group home, they made us keep data that recorded which prompt we used. There were thousands of pieces of paper that had recorded V, G or P at each notation by the task analysis. Then at the end of the month we had to calculate per task a percentage indicating the *intensity* of prompt necessary. Then we would record on an interim report, skill acquisition and prompt requirements. This information would then be further calculated in numerical terms for the annual report. While we were doing this we were like accountants at tax time. Of course we didn't have time to spend with people with disabilities, don't be absurd. It's much more important to know how Gerry responds to our fifteen minutes of teaching a day than to work at actually engaging him in life for the other 23 3/4 hours! But I digress.

Verbal prompts means that you prompt, verbally. (Some of this stuff is tough to make tough.) All it means is that for the required outcome (successful task completion) you were required to give some kind of verbal instruction. These I think are so natural that it's hard to even notice. We all teach others all the time and usually we use a lot of verbal prompting. When my niece, charming girl that she is, was teaching me how to use the computer she sat beside me and slowly gave me instructions. She did just fine until she stared at me in terror and hopelessness when I spent five minutes looking for the *Any* key. The screen told me clearly that I was to "strike any key."

I could find the Alt key, the Ins key and the Fn key,

but the *Any* key just evaded me. How was I to know that *Any* key meant any key? I thought an *Any* key was a special key called *Any*. I thought the *Any* key had been a very very bad key and we were to strike it into submission. To me, as I explained to Erin, this is a needlessly violent act and the little *Any* key probably just needs a more supportive home environment with proper nutrition and loads of love. Erin, having the patience of a typical teenager with their bulging and bumbling relatives, actually shouted at me using impolite language. You guessed it, I mistook her for the curser!

Once I figured out what the hell she was talking about, we were fine. Erin learned to teach me using simple language. Whenever I would ask her a question which would require her to answer using words like "bytes," when they don't mean mouthfuls of gooey sweet stuff, she smiles and says, "It's all just magic." And I go happily on my way.

While I remember this with fondness, it is important to note that a verbal prompt means nothing if the person has no idea what you are saying. The earlier section on instruction giving is really important now. Knowing what someone knows, is really important now. Understanding their learning style is really important now. We are for the first time talking about the actual interactions you are having with the person. Up until now we have been discussing teaching preparedness. Developing rapport, analyzing a task, then determining teaching order and the need for direct modelling is your work. The first time you open your mouth and begin actually teaching, the activity becomes interactive. Becoming prepared means that you have a clear understanding of *both* the *task* and the *person*. Your first verbal prompt, then, will reflect this knowledge in clear words and respectful tone.

When using verbal prompts, then, they need to be clear, short and address one movement at a time. "Pick up the toothpaste and then twist off the cap and put it by the sink." Is a clear prompt but it has too many steps in it. The reason you are prompting is to give a quick bit of assistance so keep it short.

Gestural prompting is prompting though gestures. When I was visiting a friend recently, I watched the most amazing teaching session. She has a young child, Susan, who has Down Syndrome. She told me that teaching her daughter was just sheer joy. This is something you rarely hear about teaching people with a significant learning handicap! As we were going out for lunch she got Susan's coat and Sue popped it on with no problem at all. Mom looked at me and said, we learned arms first!

POP QUIZ: What is her teaching strategy?

Yep, she is using forward chaining! Then they were on to the buttons. Mom kneeled down in front of Susan and put her right finger in Susan's top buttonhole and held

Susan's coat right below the top button. Then she started tickling and Sue giggled herself silly. "You know how to stop the tickle monster don't you?" Sue struggled but she got the top button into the top button hole. Then Mom put her finger in the next hole and started again. By the time they were finished, Sue had her coat done up.

This was brilliant teaching, Sue's mom knew how to prompt, she was pointing at the next hole with one finger and indicating the correct button with the other hand. And it was fun. We were all laughing by the time Sue was dressed. "The trick," Sue's mom said, "is to teach without teaching."

I understood what she meant but thought it sad that *teaching* and *learning* are *labour* words, while *play* and *laughter* are *leisure* words. I think Sue's mom was kind of diminishing her own skills and the delightful and educational process that she had developed. By using gestural prompts she ensured success and taught a skill while avoiding frustration. It's true that Susan took longer than a typical kid to do the buttons, it's true that it would have been quicker just to do it herself, but it's also true that Sue needs to learn slowly and well. This happens only when frustration is kept at bay.

Gestural prompts are like the lubrication of learning, they keep the process running smoothly. Verbal prompts can be very limiting in and of themselves and require a fair degree of linguistic skill from the learner. Gestural prompts make the assistance quite concrete.

Physical prompts are prompts that are physical. These are the most problematic of the prompt types. This involves direct physical contact with the individual. When I got into the field, using physical prompts was neither controversial nor concerning. I remember well teaching a young man, on an all male ward of an institution, how to hand wash. I stood behind him, wrapped my arms around him, took hold of his hands and wrists and gently guided him through the procedure. I was taught to use *graduated guidance* which meant fading out the support by guiding his hands through the entire process and then moving my hands up to his wrists then forearms until my support was no longer necessary.

I would *never* ... let me say this again ... *NEVER* ... again ... **NEVER** do that again. I know more now than I did then and I know now that what I did was a violation of space which involved some force (if he moved his hands away I would guide them back to tasks using gentle but firm pressure) and did not involve consent (even though he couldn't speak, in the traditional sense, I never once asked him if it would be OK to touch him). Please understand that I am not making a confession about a mistake that *I* made, I am confessing to a mistake that *we* made.

With the appropriate rise in concern about abuse of people with disabilities and confusion about staff roles, I think we need to look at how we do what we do. Using hand over hand is often necessary when beginning to teach someone whose learning style doesn't allow them to learn from verbal or gestural cues. To know this you would have had to *Stop* what you were doing and *Watch* the client learn. I think it is important that if we are going to use techniques that bring ourselves into contact with the bodies of the people we serve, we should have documented somewhere that less intrusive kinds of prompting were tried and were found to be ineffective. This serves to legitimize our use of physical prompts.

If you are going to use a physical prompt, it is important to try to situate yourself so that you aren't hugging the person. By teaching at the side, or best, from the front, you can teach using the maximum amount of touch needed for the hand over hand teaching and yet minimize the direct body contact with the person.

I know I am going to get in trouble for saying this but often hand over hand training is done for people who have some fairly significant disabilities. I wonder how many of the skills that we are teaching them this way are really necessary. First we need to adapt as much as possible. Use Velcro instead of shoe laces and shoe tying becomes a snap, or rather a ripping success. Use a soft soap instead of a slippery bar and lathering up becomes easy. Sideways learners need sideways approaches. I understand completely teaching the basic skills of hygiene and dressing to someone as it gives a greater degree of dignity and ableness to that person. Too, it then no longer necessitates that a staff provide them close physical care.

BUT. Other functional stuff, bed making, table setting, seem such dreary goals for someone to expend a ton of effort in acquiring. I'm sorry but it takes a staff four seconds to do these things and it's going to take years of programming and a thousand hand over hand sessions to teach these things and at the end what do you have? A poorly made bed and a table looking like it was set by Jim Carrey on a bad day.

Maybe we should teach what's necessary and then teach what's fun. Teaching someone who has a significant disability to play a simple computer game that makes cool noises when a point is scored will give hours of pleasure. Way more pleasure than looking at a well set table, I'd wager. Teaching someone to give a high five, a low five and an on the side five in greeting to friends can be hysterically funny. Way funnier than a bed that you are just going to mess up again anyways.

I know we have been taught to teach the functional, but I advocate teaching the fun-tional. I know people are going to say that I'm demeaning people with disabilities but I don't think I am. It's just that if hours of work are going to go into teaching something, shouldn't it make a real difference in the quality of life of the person. And I'm real sorry table setting, shoe tying and bed making are real quality of life issues for me. Again, I am writing this for those individuals who will take very long periods of time to learn something. After my near death experience this year I realized that the time we have is *all we have*. Four years of teaching bed making is four years of someone's *life* and it's the only *life* they have.

(If you decide to abandon these as teaching *goals*, please re-read the section on Apprenticeship. My suggestion here is not to disengage people from life expectations, it is simply to ensure that we focus *time* and *energy* on things that make sense.)

The use of physical prompting usually means that it's going to take a long time to teach someone something. So if you are going to have to physically take someone's hand to teach them where to put a knife on a table ... recognize that by the time you are done they will be two or three years older and will have spent much of that time wanting to put the knife in your back. Is it worth it? To them? To you? Or should you sit down and figure out some social or leisure skill that will make a huge difference in their lives?

Just asking.

Tool# 10: Repetition

Repetition is necessary but boring. Repetition is necessary but boring. Repetition is necessary but boring. If I do this one more time I'll fall asleep at the keyboard! I am very aware that every class that is ever taught about teaching people with disabilities mentions the need for repetition. What they need to say over and over again is that repetition doesn't work if it's boring. Repetition can be fun!! Who can learn if they are bored silly. Doing stuff in different ways can be exhilarating. In fact, the last thing that anyone can do while falling asleep is learn to make a bed!! But if a difficult task is approached from different ways it can actually seem like a fresh new start. (You will note, of course, that I began this paragraph by saying the same thing over three times in exactly the same way. You will then note that I ended the paragraph by saying the same thing over three times but in entirely different words. Your experience as a reader, I'll bet, was quite different given the different approach to repetition.)

Too often our approach to repetition is to take a difficult task and make the person do it over and over again. This is education from education hell. Repetition really means doing the same thing over but in different ways using different learning strategies. When I teach about body parts I first use an anatomically correct doll and have the class name the parts. Then I get up and draw the outline of two bodies and ask the class to tell me what I need to draw on the bodies to make them into either an adult woman or an adult man. Then I show a film where a man and a woman each with a developmental disability teach about body parts. Exactly the same concept taught in three entirely different ways. Repetition done well (if I may blow my own horn here) doesn't *feel* like the same thing at all.

Tool # 11: Feedback

Feedback. There is a term I have come to hate. You know, when your supervisor brings you in the office to share with you, you know it ain't coffee and a donut. Feedback is supposed to be helpful information upon which we can change our behaviours for the better. Yeah, right. If that's so how come it's usually given by those in positions of power to those in a subordinate position. Have you ever given your supervisor feedback? And didn't it sound kind of like this ...

"Oh yes, oh wonderful and brilliant creature of God, your very time in my humble life just adds so much!!" I call this the hind lick manoeuvre. It removes blockages and breathes life into my career on a regular basis!! I once had a supervisor who went to a training about giving constructive feedback. She learned a three to one ratio. She learned, from some management guru, that she was supposed to say three positive things to one negative thing. So when going into her office all her staff learned to count and if she started out by saying something nice our stomachs fell to our ankles. If she continued by complimenting something we were wearing, panic sped the heartbeat. By the third nice little compliment, we knew we were in really big trouble. Yeah, feedback is just great.

Feedback, used properly, should have absolutely no emotional impact. It's just information after all. The fact that we cringe in the face of criticism means that we have learned to associate feedback with a personal attack or as evidence of personal failure. Feedback to be effective has to

70

be non-judgemental. It needs to clearly separate the *individual* from the *attempt*. Look at the two following sentences said in two very different teaching styles. Gail is attempting to learn to put on her sweater.

> *That is wonderful, Gail, you tried very hard. I like it when you try on your own. Now let me check your buttons. All right but one! Wow, you must have really paid attention. See how this top button is out of line. Let's fix it.*

Compare this to another style all together:

> *Gwen you know you aren't supposed to put your sweater on until I'm there. Your sweater is buttoned up all wrong. Get over here and I will fix it for you.*

In both situations the sweater wasn't quite right. In the first situation, though, Gwen was given information about how to fix the problem. But the staff recognized something of tremendous importance. Initiative. Gwen learned a lot. She learned that effort is valuable, that in-dependence is a good thing, that concentration pays off and that support people will help when she needs it.

In the second situation the staff saw the *problem* was initiative. What did Gwen think she was trying to do anyways? Keep up that level of non-compliance and self-reliance and she just might be able to fire the staff one day. God forbid she try to be independent of us.

My trouble with feedback is keeping the judgement out and focusing just on information. Further, adding a bit of honest praise into the mix makes it really difficult. Sometimes when I'm at work I open my mouth and my mother's voice comes out. We have to unlearn so much in our jobs!! (Oh, it's lower in tone but it's definitely my mother's voice. Sorry Ma, but I still remember the spots on the dishes speech. And, Ma, for your information I never did learn to make my bed properly. So there.)

So you think this is easy? How many of you had a father who praised your hair by saying, "At least it doesn't look like a rat's nest?" Try a little exercise. The numbered sentences which follow all need changing into something a little more non-judgemental.

1.   How many times have I told you that the washing machine is downstairs? THIS is the dishwasher!

2.   You dressed yourself!! I take it your top half is going to Alaska and your bottom half is going to Florida?

3.   I'm so glad you peed standing up. I see you've learned to do your initials on the bath mat.

Go ahead and try, it can be done! Don't start teaching until you can do this kind of thing easily.

Tool # 12: Praise

This is where you get to whip up some enthusiasm for the entire process. Not only that! You can whip up confidence and self esteem. But most importantly you can whip up determination. My mother-in-law once said that for her the two most important ingredients in success are intuitiveness and "stick-to-it-iveness." The simple act of praise can teach both. (Yes, you can teach intuitiveness by honouring a personal process of learning! And "stick-to-it-iveness" comes from a sense of successful journey. Oh Ye doubters!)

People love to work for praise and acknowledgement. A study done here in Canada asked office workers to list their main considerations in choosing a job and then their main considerations for staying in a job. Money ranked in the top five when people were asked what they thought about when choosing a job. For staying in a job though, money fell out of the top ten altogether. The number one issue was "working for an honest and ethical company" and number two was "feeling that my input is acknowledged and appreciated."

Praise and your willingness to praise effort is the most important teaching tool. It does something that none of the other tools here does. It encourages risk. All learning involves risk. It also communicates acceptance. Even so, this can be the most difficult of the tools to use. With practice it can become entirely natural.

Praise to be effective as a teaching tool, has to have

three simple components. First, it has to be meant. By now this should not be difficult. After doing a task analysis and then watching the individual attempt to learn, it is easy to see effort and if you can squint your eyes you will see a miracle too. (Remember, people with disabilities are widely believed to be uneducable, when they learn right in front of you, recognize what you are seeing!) Keeping this in mind it becomes easier to tell the person what it is you are feeling. What person wouldn't find this praise exhilarating.

> *Gee Sky, I sure appreciate you trying so hard. You make me very proud.*

Second, it has to be personal. Generic praise is insufficient. In order to be personal it has to reflect what is happening. A person who has just tied their first bow doesn't understand, "That's nice." In fact, generic praise is often patronizing. In order to monogram praise you need to state the achievement, the circumstance and your feeling.

> *A tidy room! All by yourself! You have made my day!!!*

Clear, personal praise will be remembered long after it is given.

Finally, it has to be used. Praise, when we first start using it is rusty; over time it becomes burnished. With each use we become more comfortable and we are more likely to try again. The difficulty at first is determining when to use it. The answer is as simple as it is complex. Use it whenever you see success. Learning to see success is another story. Most of us have been forced by a competitive world to see success in terms of perfection rather than in terms of effort and struggle. This inhibits praise. If one can only praise that which is perfect, one will seldom praise.

Support people need to learn to see an individual's smudged, occasionally wrinkled successes. This may mean praising a small part of a large task or a less than perfect, full hearted attempt at a whole job. Each is a bona fide accomplishment.

This is not natural!! Years ago when I was going to university I would go every Wednesday to the cathedral downtown for an hour or so. The first time I went I discovered quite a little crowd. There was also clearly an etiquette to this kind of thing. I noted this by arriving at about three o'clock and found at about three fifteen two older women arrive and hover behind where I sat in the back pew and begin to mutter about their spot being taken. I got up discreetly as if I was going to the candle lighting area and they dove into place. It didn't take a scholar to figure that newcomers sit near the front and old timers have their spots at the back.

After a few weeks an old nun changed her seating pattern and began sitting in the row behind me just off to my right. One day she belted me (I didn't know that nun's could pack such a punch) and said, "You pray for me, I'll pray for you, God likes it better that way." Sister Mary

Holy Cross (I'd swear on a stack of bibles that was the name she gave me.) One day I was coming back to Victoria from Vancouver and was surprised to see Sister Mary on the boat. We chatted and I offered to drive her back to Victoria which I thought would be better than taking the bus in and then a taxi from the bus stop. She agreed and when the boat docked we walked off the boat and over to the parking area where I had left my car. Sister Mary wouldn't let me drive until she had said enough Hail Mary's to make up for an adolescent male's nightly sin. Putting the rosary away she said, "You can drive now." I still think the bus company should have thanked me for taking her off their hands!

On our way back in the car driving at nun speed which is somewhere between stop and the rate grass grows, she told me why she had been in Vancouver. She was at a celebration of her fiftieth year of being a nun. Fifty years can form quite a habit!! I asked her if it was fun. She said, "It was nice to hear so many nice things said about me. I didn't know that what I had done had been so well appreciated." I told her that she should be proud of her accomplishments. She said, "I think life wouldn't have been so hard sometimes if they had spread all those nice things out over the years rather than waiting fifty years to say them." Amen Sister!

And by the way, congratulations for making it through the longest chapter of the book. It's clear sailing from here on. And hey ... I mean that.

Chapter 5
967 - Eleven Eleven

She wasn't supposed to be able to learn anything. She had a fairly severe disability, didn't respond very well to our teaching programs, and wasn't particularly motivated. One evening, sitting in the front room all alone she began singing in a gentle lilt a tune we all knew well, "♫967-Eleven Eleven.♫ Even sitting here writing this that little tune dances in my head like spring elves dancing amongst the morning dew, like water sprites swirling to soft ethereal tunes, like dove footprints which dance over freshly fallen snow. I know that this little song will catch in my brain and stay there for hours. I love all the words to the song too. Join me as we sing: ♫ 967♫ Eleven Eleven♫ phone pizza pizza ♫ Woah oh oh ♫ phone pizza pizza♫ Woah oh oh.♫ Ah, who needs Oh Do Wah Ditty Ditty Dum Ditty Doo when one has fast food jingles? How about this good ol' song, "Two all beef patties, special sauce, lettuce, cheese ..." or "When you eat your smarties do you eat the red ones last, do you crunch them very slowly or munch them very fast?" and the classic, "Oh, I wish I were An Oscar Myer Wiener, that is what I'd truly like to be - e - e..." Gosh, I love a good sing-a-long.

After about a week of us figuring that it was pretty damn cute that Melanie could sing the pizza phone number we realized that she had *learned* the phone number. Melanie who we couldn't teach. Melanie whose learning skills were so "low" that we couldn't make a task analysis with small enough baby steps. Melanie whose program binder had definitely been on a low cal diet of good ideas for a very long time. This very same Melanie had learned, "♫967♫ Eleven♫Eleven♫phone pizza pizza.♫ Some *tie and suit* advertising executive in some tall building somewhere in downtown Toronto had managed to teach numbers to a young woman with a severe learning handicap.

"Yeah, but it's useless because it's meaningless." We comforted ourselves with this for a while. Until one of the staff taught Melanie to punch those numbers on the phone. "Yeah, but how is that going to help her in her everyday life." We continued to diminish what Melanie had learned until one of the new staff said, "Maybe we should figure out how Melanie managed to learn those numbers." The answer as it turned out was that Melanie loved simple tunes. We didn't know that because, while there was music on in the house most of the time, the music she heard was complex rock/pop music. Music that staff liked. Music that wasn't particularly hummable. Music that was *age appropriate*.

You should meet Melanie now, her verbal skills have increased. As verbal skills they are a tad ... odd ... but they are definitely verbal skills. If you go into her home you will be greeted appropriately and slightly musically with a nice, "♫♫Hello, there!♫♫" At the dinner table she responds well with either a "♫♫Yes Please♫♫" or a "♫♫No Thanks♫♫♫ Staff now find teaching her much more fun. She still has tremendous difficulty learning basics like bed making and shoe tying, but she can and does learn to appropriately verbalize wants and needs. I know, I know, that she sometimes sits and sings these little ditties to herself. And I know that some staff have been bugged by the "self stim" nature of her quiet musings. Yep, and I also know that some of the normalization folks have thought that what she did was immature and childlike. But I also know that the quality of her life has improved. I know, too, that for the first time Melanie enjoys learning and the staff enjoy teaching her. Never has more active planning gone on in the staff's minds regarding what little tunes they can teach her next. It's odd that when we learn to do things the way they need to be done for a person with a disability, there is someone somewhere who finds it politically insulting? I guess it will always be easier to write a philosophy than teach a skill.

But the real question here is, why did Melanie learn that damn phone number? The real answer? It was fun!!! By discovering something she liked, did naturally and repeated without prompting we found a "way in" to Melanie's learning style. Over time we have come to use some ...

Learning Strategies that Are Fun (the title the publisher thought should be used. Would you want to have dinner with someone this verbally sparkling?)

There are two formal approaches that I'd like to tell you about and then there are some examples of what some folks have done that have really impressed me. One of the formal approaches which is highly fun, motivating and successful, I have mentioned in almost every book I have ever written. I mention it again.

Video Self Modelling is an approach developed by Dr. Peter Dowrick and has the potential to revolutionize teaching people with developmental disabilities.

Let's look at a problem that people with disabilities often have and then look at why what Dr. Dowrick did is so important. First, look at the fact that people with disabilities have difficulty with abstraction. Second, look at the fact that most of our teaching processes involve a lot of wordy instructions. Third, look at the fact that words are by definition abstract. Now, consider what we think is happening when we are teaching someone something. We imagine that the words are pouring out of our mouths and into their ears and that something significant is happening with those words.

Have you ever responded to someone giving you directions to do something by saying, "I see?" When you said that, what did you mean? In reality "I see" does not mean "I understand" or "I get it now" or "Ah ha." "I see" means "I see". It means that you actually can picture what those words mean. This is highly evolved abstraction.

Have you ever taught someone to, say, control their temper? Have you ever, then, noticed that they can tell you exactly what they should do in certain situations but they never do it? Well, why is that? Often we figure that they are being willfully non-compliant. Maybe there is a different explanation. Maybe what is happening is that they haven't learned it at all. Let's be honest, we judge a person's under-standing of what we have said by their ability to repeat what we have said. Therefore, I believe that most people with disabilities listen to repeat rather than listen to comprehend. Like Melanie singing, "♬ 967 ♬ Eleven ♬ Eleven ♬," it's meaningless until she learned to use the phone. So instead of figuring that they *know* but *don't do*, maybe they *don't do* because they *don't know*.

This is where video self modelling comes in. Dr. Dowrick suggests that we make a video of what we are trying to teach. Let's take a situation that required a lot of complex teaching. We were working with a guy who when he got aroused he stopped thinking. (This makes him a pretty typical male.) As he enjoyed homosexual contact, bathrooms in public places were pretty difficult for him. For you it may be a row of men at urinals, for him it was a buffet. He had learned, by rote, the following solution, "When I am horny in the bathroom I need to leave the bathroom and find a staff to help me." Beyond potentially leaving him dependant on staff for support, he never did this in the situation.

Here's what we did. We sat down and wrote a script that would have him look at the camera, say, "Hi, my name is Eric. I am going to show how to control myself." Then he would walk into a bathroom, the camera would focus on him coming in to the washroom. Then the camera would swing to a staff standing at the urinal pretending to pee. Then the camera would swing back to Eric. At this point a tape recording would be turned on. This tape played a pre-recorded message that Eric had done saying, "I am in the bathroom. I am horny. This is a public place. I don't have sex in public places." Then after the tape played, Eric turned and left the washroom. The final scene was Eric standing outside the washroom looking at the camera and saying, "My name is Eric, I am in control and proud of myself."

This takes only a few minutes to write but took quite a while to film and edit. But! The first time he saw the film Eric actually said, "Oh, I see!!" We were sailing now. Eric was understanding for the first time the complex set of skills that he needed to perform. This procedure was used to teach Eric a variety of other skills regarding sexuality, impulsivity and consent. Complex stuff for a guy, who never got it when we taught using other methods.

This method is fun, engaging and highly motivating for the individual! For further information about setting up a program like this take a look for an article by Betsy Benson in the Habilitative Mental Healthcare Newsletter.

Game Approaches are fun! Behaviour Management Services has done a lot of work in the area of teaching social skills. One of their consulting psychologists, Dr. Quinsey, had used a game approach to teaching social skills to men

82

in prison. The idea caught fire. They found that one of the best methods of teaching social skills was by developing a game that made learning fun, had tons of opportunities for practice and that could be done on a casual basis in a group home. What they did was come up with a series of questions that targeted specific needs and then turned these into game cards. The individuals playing the game then would be learning while socializing and having a ton of fun.

The idea that learning can be a social activity and that social activities should be learned in a social setting was revolutionary. They have, I believe, come to understand that learning approaches for people with disabilities should be "marked" by their spark of creativity.

I talked with Susan Tough, the director of Behaviour Management Services, about the Social Skills game. I was telling her how impressed I was with the game and she said that she worked on and with the game almost from the beginning. The whole concept of learning through playing shouldn't be a surprise. One only needs to realize that one of the reasons that there are so many games for children and sports opportunities for slightly older children is that society believes that these activities teach a set of values to children. In the United States, one of the ways they are attacking the gang and drug subculture is by having Midnight Basketball games. The creation of a fun activity for others to learn how to relate is not a novel idea.

What's novel here is the recognition that people with

disabilities need the same kind of opportunities to learn. The use of the Social Skills game make people with disabilities *more like* not *less like* other learners. Susan told me of a number of situations that happened in the social skills game she either ran or supervised. Interestingly, her favourite stories involved a lot of humour and laughing not learning and struggling. Interesting concept, huh?

So looking at turning something difficult to teach into a fun activity makes sense. It makes even more sense to develop an approach wherein a number of people are learning at the same time. In order to do this you might want to look at the social skills game and read its rules carefully. They have thought this through quite thoroughly and much can be learned by it. You can contact them at York Behaviour Management Services, 10 Trench Street, Richmond Hill, Ontario, Canada L4C 4Z3. (I hate putting this kind of thing into a reference list.)

The *creative spark* should mark almost all of our teaching. I know myself when working with a young man who had some difficulty understanding boundaries, I noticed that when left alone he would sit and draw. He had an interesting approach to art because whatever he drew he drew from a perspective of above and back a bit, like he was looking down on the scene. In a moment's inspiration we decided that he could draw himself and appropriate boundaries into a little book that he could use to teach himself. Why not go from strength?

A while ago I was asked to sit in on a fellow who was teaching his first class on AIDS prevention to a group of adults with developmental disabilities. He had noticed that they had a great deal of trouble with understanding the highly abstract concept of infection and contagion. The day I joined he did something for the first time. He brought into the group a paper bag and then quite unexpectedly pulled a water pistol out of the bag and began to shoot it at all the members of the class. They went into hysterics. Me too, it was funny. Then while chatting he took out a condom rolled it over the gun and then shot at them. He pointed out that the condom protected them.

Brilliant. Sheer, awesome, brilliance. The creative spark at work.

In working in the sexuality clinic we constantly have to come up with ways of teaching difficult concepts. Once working with a guy who had come out of the prison system, I was shocked to find that this guy was able, very well able, to use cognitive thought stopping as a technique to deal with his sexual urges. In talking, he attributed his ability to the therapist he had in the correctional system.

With his permission I called the therapist and asked, "How did you teach such a difficult cognitive strategy to someone with a tough learning disability?" He laughed. That, I have learned, is a real good sign. He told me that he tried something new with Frank. He said that Frank could feel himself losing control and which showed that Frank recognized, identified and understood feelings. So he took him to the gym when there was no one else there, sat Frank in a wheel chair and then put some huge padded rolls up against the gym wall. He then took the wheelchair from behind and said to Frank, "You yell stop when we are getting too close." Then he ran towards the padding while Frank laughed uproariously. The first time they tumbled into the big padded tubes. The second time Frank yelled stop just in time. For the rest of that session Frank did very well at yelling, "Stop!" Then the next session he brought in the kind of stop sign that crossing guards use. He gave the sign to Frank and said, "This time when we are getting too close hold the sign up in front of you. Frank did it right the first time out. They both enjoyed the session and Frank even put the therapist in the wheelchair and gave him the stop sign. Role play is fun but in this case Frank wasn't so good at Roll Play and didn't stop well. But it didn't matter because it was fun.

Then they moved on to Frank just raising his hand and imagining the stop sign being in it. They did this using imagination one time, the stop sign the next. This went on for several sessions. Then Frank graduated to just imagination. From there in sessions the therapist taught him to use his imagination to see the stop sign whenever he was feeling out of control and about to crash.

I was, as I hope you are, awestruck. It's nice to bask for a second in genius, huh? Even a small creative spark can be pretty damn illuminating!

The creative spark can be seen in goal selection too. (If this section seems like it was added on at the last minute, it was. I got back from a trip wherein I had a conversation with someone about a teaching program that they had just finished and was so amazed by what they'd done I had to add it to the book. Trouble was finding where to put their example. The discussion of *creativity* seemed to be the best place for it.) When *creativity* combines with *compassion* the outcome is often a high *calibre* of service.

Dianne lives in a service agency and managed to annoy pretty much everyone who worked with her. She constantly asked staff, *Are you happy?* Or, *Are you mad?* Or, *Happy, now?* Or, *Mad, now?* They decided to program this annoying behaviour away, and being good little behaviourists they knew that you don't take one behaviour away without giving another back. So, they were teaching her alternative conversation starters. She was learning to talk about things like the weather. Should Dianne ever get stuck on the elevator, she'll do well!

Trouble was the program was working. Dianne was asking staff fewer questions but wasn't using many of the other conversation starters. Too, the staff noticed that Dianne was growing increasingly anxious and as a means of dealing with her anxiety she spent more and more time in her room. A couple months later one of the staff was in the agency library browsing around through their journals while waiting for a meeting with her supervisor. She came across an interesting article which said that a lot of people with disabilities had difficulty with recognition of feelings in others.

This fact sat in her mind for about a month and suddenly, in an instant, she understood what Dianne was doing. Imagine that you had difficulty in recognizing the feelings of others. Wouldn't this cause you a great deal of stress and anxiety? Being around people whose feelings were *invisible* to you would be horrible. Just think about it, facial expressions would happen but you wouldn't know what they meant. Someone's voice tone would change inexplicably. Wouldn't you feel absolutely lost socially? Perhaps Dianne was asking about staff feelings as a means of checking out her social environment. Perhaps her goal was to reassure herself that all was OK. Perhaps the program was increasing her anxiety because it was taking away from her an *adaptive skill* that made up for a disability related impairment.

The staff stopped the programming entirely and put her on a program aimed at teaching her how to read facial expressions and understand tone of voice. They aimed broadly at teaching about *happy* and *angry* as these were the two that she asked about most constantly. As Dianne was learning, they let her ask as many times as she wanted. Interestingly, the staff no longer found this annoying as they understood the source of the behaviour. Over time Dianne learned to read some basic social cues and the *feelings-asking behaviour* diminished. They noticed that she, during times of confusion, will ask more than at times of calm but that isn't seen as a problem at all. It's seen as a *normal* kind of thing for someone to do.

Even though this example fits uncomfortably into this part of the book, I really wanted to write it down. This teaching was brilliant. It was creative, it took into consideration the disability and it worked to address a real problem. The problem of course wasn't *question asking* it was *difficulty with feelings recognition*.

I have become convinced that every time we sit down to devise a plan to teach a person with a significant learning handicap a skill we need to check and see if our creative spark is bright enough to fire inspiration.

Chapter 6
Doing Data

I know that this chapter title sounds like a little song that some of the crew members on the Enterprise might sing. But I'm afraid it's a tad duller than that. In fact data is often hard to collect, easy to lose and meaningless to most. This is a tragedy. Perhaps I am way wrong but I think far too much paper is wasted in human services. It is my contention that the human service system was created to support people with disabilities and now we spend most of our time supporting the system and not people with disabilities.

In fact, my own relationship with paperwork is legend in all agencies that I have ever worked for. I stayed at Behaviour Management Services as a full time consultant for two years longer than I wanted to. Why? Because I knew it would take me an entire year to just bring my files up to date. Now I just tell people right off that I am organizationally impaired and let it go at that. So why would a person who sees paper as processed dead tree bodies suggest the taking of data? Well, simply because data, used properly, actually means something. The trouble is we usually take data about the wrong things. As I mentioned earlier I was made to take data that recorded the type of assistance that someone needed on a step of the task analysis. I tried and tried and tried to get people to understand that we were taking data on the process not on the product. This issue isn't what kind of teaching prompts were used on a particular day. The issue is how does the person perform the overall skill? In fact, people were so obsessed with this kind of stuff that the data got in the way of the teaching. To teach hand washing, for example, we would have to take the binder into the bathroom have pen in hand and at every step of the task record what was going on. Only part of our attention was on teaching, all the rest of our attention was on issues like...

☞   Where's the pen?

☞   I think I used both a physical and gestural prompt how do you mark that?

☞   Gosh she went ahead two steps and I'm not sure she did it right. I know!! I'll put down independent.

☞   Gosh the paper got wet! I wish she'd just slow down!!

☞   How did the pen get there!?!

☞   Darn! The pen went through the wet paper.

This doesn't make sense. I think what makes more sense is to record the product not the process. Taking daily data on tasks we are teaching is simply a waste of time. Moreover, how well could you perform if each time you tried something someone was standing beside you writing it in a little book? The simple act of recording causes change in behaviour. I remember reading a report about a sexual survey that had participants mark in a calendar every time they had sex. Several of the couples felt compelled to ensure that there were lots of marks on the calendar and ended up having to drop out of the survey. Seems friction had worn the men down to little nubs and the women were upset because they weren't getting much else done!! So data affects performance, make no mistake.

A preferred process would be to record performance on every fifth or sixth trial. This means that the teacher and learner get the opportunity to work unencumbered by the process of taking data. Then on the day data is taken teaching stops. On this day the person is asked to perform the task and only minimal assistance is given when necessary. This day is not an instructional day so the typical style of feedback and prompting is not used. In this process the only thing that matters is performance, and all that is measured is successful com-pletion or prompt necessary. This information is easily compiled on a data form that acts as both to compile and graph daily data. It's ease of use makes it a preferred tool for taking data on any skill that utilizes a task analysis. Since we are looking here at teaching, I am only going to present this one style of data collection. (In the final instalment of this "behaviour series" of books, there will be much more emphasis on data.) If you were collecting data on a variety of other kinds of behaviours there are many other kinds of forms. This one's use is limited to teaching. The form looks like this:

Name: _Serge_

Week of: _Oct. 23, 1999_

TASK	date:	Oct 23	Oct 24	Oct 25	Oct 26	Oct 27	Total
18.	Open eyes						5
17.	Breathe quietly						1
16.	"I feel calm"						5
15.	Relax face						2
14.	Scrunch face						2
13.	Lower shoulders						4
12.	Raise shoulders						4
11.	Lower arms						5
10.	Raise arms						5
9.	Relax stomach						0
8.	Pull in stomach						1
7.	Set feet down						5
6.	Raise feet floor						2
5.	Relax foot						5
4.	Arch foot						5
3.	Take breaths						2
2.	Close eyes						4
1.	Sit upright...						5
TOTAL		8	11	12	15	17	

☐ Assistance Needed   ◩ Correctly Done   ◪ Total

94

This particular graph will allow you to see the progress overall and be able to pick out particular steps that are problematic. Let me explain how it's done. As you can see, on the day that data is taken the person scoring the skill puts down a slash on the step wherein the person does it independently and leaves it blank where assistance was necessary. Then the scorer totals up the number of slashes and marks that number with another slash. Voilà, you have a graph. Not only do you have a graph, you have a lot of information. Take a look at the data sheet. What two this do you notice right away? Well, first off Serge is learning! Second, Serge has a lot of trouble with steps 8 and 9 as well as 14 and 15. What would you do? Ah ha, you're right maybe these steps need to be broken down further.

Pretty cool, huh? I was so bad in math in school I thought that a graph was an animal with a reeeeeeally long neck. And here I am just graphing away! And actually understanding it.

Chapter 7
Old Behaviourists Never Die:
They Just Fade Away

I don't like using reinforcement, people with disabilities get addicted to praise and then you end up having to praise them for every little thing. The woman who said this at a planning meeting was adamant that we should only use a minimal amount of praise or other forms of positive reinforcement when working with the folks in the group home. I sat there feeling guilty. I felt caught. I wanted to get up at that moment and say, "My name is Dave and I'm addicted to reinforcement."

There are some ridiculous ideas out there about reinforcement. The most dangerous of these is that reinforcement is an *undesirable* and *unnatural* aspect of human interchange. This leads many to plan to fade (behavioural term that means get rid of) all forms of reinforcement from the life of people with disabilities in their care. The idea being that none of us get reinforcement, why should they? Beyond being whiny, this idea is just plain wrong. If you counted the number of times that you received some form of reinforcement in a day you would be shocked at the size of the number. Every time someone leans towards you when you are telling a story, laughs at a joke you tell, raises their eyebrows and rolls their eyes in a moment of shared understanding, or eggs you on when you are gossiping about your boss by saying, yeah, yeah, what next, wow what a cow, you have been reinforced. Every time your arm is touched when in conversation, your hand shaken after a decision is made, you get a high five from a co-worker, you have been reinforced. Every time you open your pay check, well perhaps I go too far, but you get the idea.

I remember writing teaching programs for people with disabilities knowing that reinforcement would be powerful because the individuals lived in a state of *reinforcer poverty*. Even so, I was taught that a program wasn't over until the reinforcement was returned to a *natural* level. It didn't occur to me that we were *beginning* the teaching program with people who lived with an *unnaturally* low number of reinforcements. Oh well, realization that comes late is still realization. Now I realize that the idea of *fading* reinforcers is kind of dangerous. We need to recognize that we will be increasing the level of reinforcement while we are teaching but we also need to recognize that we need to *reduce* but not *eliminate* reinforcers. We need to return them to a *natural* level of reinforcement.

If it shocks you to hear me say that getting reinforcement is *natural*, then you really need to think about your life. I have learned that people with disabilities aren't the only ones who sometimes live with a dearth of reinforcers. When I was in the hospital, during the writing of this book, the doctors weren't sure I would survive the illness. Once they had determined that I would live but that the recovery would be difficult, I was out of that bed faster than chocolate melts, while every step was pain wracked, I walked every day. I refused to be toileted in bed. (Please! Fitting me on a bedpan would be akin to docking the Titanic at a parking meter) Though they suggested I not walk for a week I walked the six feet from the bed to the bathroom twice a day. No cold bedpans for me!

On my third day of walking, the doctor came, pulled the curtain around me and asked, "What got you out of bed and walking?" I was surprised by the question and said, "The more I walk the sooner I get better, get home, get back to work." He shook his head saying, "There are so many people in here no where near as sick as you are and we can't get them out of bed. It's like this is a break from their life. You've got to wonder what kind of lives some people have." I thought about that a lot. I have constantly railed about the fact that people with disabilities live with so little in the way of human interaction. That they aren't valued by those around them. I wonder now. Is this part of the human condition for a lot of people? Should most of us be on regular reinforcement programs? Have most of us had our reinforcement faded down to nil? Do we live starving for notice and attention?

There are things you need to think about here. First, do you get enough reinforcement in your life? If the answer is "Yes," then ask yourself what it would be like to lose it or have it fade away. If the answer is "No," then ask yourself two questions. First, ain't it awful? If there were anything you could do to ensure that others get the attention and reinforcement, shouldn't you do it? Second, how can you increase the amount of reinforcement that you get in your life? For me, I realized that I crawled along a hospital corridor, holding on to a walker, enduring incredible pain only because I wanted to get back to a life wherein I do get reinforcement. In some ways I think that my life was saved by a drive for reinforcement. Overstating it? Perhaps. (I think the thoughts and prayers of others helped too.)

Alright it's important but what is it?

Reinforcement simply stated, is anything that increases a behaviour.

(Sorry for the interruption, I allow myself 10 minutes of playing Wordtris for every 5 pages I write -- now where were we -- oh yeah we were talking about reinforcement.)

To use reinforcement effectively for teaching a behaviour we need to find out what the person likes. There are a number of different kinds of reinforcers. There are basically six different categories of reinforcers. When beginning a teaching program it pays to spend a bit of time getting to know the likes and dislikes of the learner. Learning what they like teaches you what motivates them. We are all driven or pulled by desires for a variety of things, activities, opportunities or experiences. This is no less true because a person has a disability.

100

Reinforcers and How to Use Them
(My Editor's Kindly But Dull Idea for a Chapter Title)

Types of Reinforcers:

When looking for what may serve as reinforcers for someone, just imagine that they could drive and you were driving behind them. If they had one of those *I* ♡ bumper stickers, what would it say? There are basically six different *I* ♡ categories:

I ♡ *to eat ...*

This category of reinforcers is the easiest to figure out. Just ask the person out for lunch and then let them choose. And do it on petty cash, hey this is work!! If they can't tell you there will be a ton of people who will know their favourite snacks, meals, or drinks. This category of reinforcer is so easy to use, but oddly it upsets some folks. I once went out for dinner with my parents, sister-in-law and niece. It was a fancy-smanchy Chinese restaurant in Victoria. My niece was uncontrollable. She did all those things that make men think that "vasectomy" is a French word for "hell of a good idea." I grabbed a bunch of fortune cookies from a jar at the door. She was immediately interested in them and why not, they are sweet, they are edible, this is my gene pool we are talking here. I gave them to her a little at a time when she was quiet. When she yelled, I ate little pieces (and why not? *I* was being quiet.)

She quickly became quiet and we were enjoying playing a game with the food. (Food can be a eaten, played with, chatted to and commiserated with, ah yes.) My sister-in-law was really annoyed with me. She said that using food as a reward was treating her child no better than a dog.

Well!

First, dogs or any animal shouldn't be seen as less than humans in respect to their ability to feel and their need for respectful treatment. Second, most dogs are better behaved than my niece. Third, it wasn't like I was rubbing her face in the food she'd thrown on the carpet, not that the screaming didn't prompt me to think such nasty thoughts.

So be prepared to defend your use of these kinds of reinforcers. Your defense will have to be even stronger if the person likes stuff that is bad for them. Chocolate bars, ju jubes and the like can cause thin little people to go into cardiac arrest at the idea of candy as a reinforcer. There is always someone, somewhere, who feels that someone else shouldn't be who they are, like what they like, think what they think and do what they do. This isn't a concern in human services of course because we've all learned that we need to leave our prejudices at home and allow the people we serve to fully individuate, right?

I ♡ to do...

Quick, if you had an afternoon off from work with no

responsibilities, make a list of five things you would like to do with that time. You are probably listing a bunch of activities. Are you picturing yourself lying in a hot steamy Jacuzzi surrounded by bubbles as water swirls around your back and between your toes? Hmmm, by now I'm picturing you this way!! (Sorry, but did you know you look cute all soapy and water-wrinkled?) If not a bath taken, how about a bike ridden? A book read? A dog walked? A cat petted? A CD played? A store shopped? A wall painted? A flower gardened? A soap opera watched? The list is endless. There are things we love to do just for the joy of doing them. These are often completely free, excepting the considerable expense of time. When coming up with a list of potential reinforcers for a person with a disability, try very hard to explore this area. Almost all of these involve communion between the person and, society, music, art, self, soul. These are really cool reinforcers to use.

I ♡ to play with ...

Right now I can imagine three things happening.

1: The jackboots of the politically correct as they march to my door to inform me that it is *age inappropriate* for adults to play with toys.

2: The dirty minded saying ... *yeah, yeah, play with what? Come on, come on, are you talking about a condiment carnival?* All I have to say to your type is, "get your mind out of the butter!"

3:     Reasonable people like you and me thinking, *Oh my gosh the number of things I like to play with is just plain huge.*

Anyone here like to play Scrabble, Cribbage, Bridge, Pool? Anyone here like to play with clay, coloured markers, puppets, paper clips? Anyone here like playing with teddy bears, Barbie dolls, wooden trucks, Lego building blocks? Anyone who doesn't have *age inappropriate* activities in their repertoire is way too much an adult for my taste. A couple of months ago in Philadelphia I went into a kind of International Toys Я Us and found this neat little wire toy. You can fiddle with it and fiddle with it and it makes all sorts of different shapes. It's made with silver wire with little beads placed on each loop. I stood in the store playing with it when the clerk approached and said, "Sir, that's a toy for children." I looked blankly at her wondering if she was working a second job to implement her income from a group home. Then she said with disdain, "It's for *girls*." I bought it. And I play with it when I'm feeling particularly defiant.

Rules about age, gender and play confuse me. I kind of think that play is, well, play. And what someone plays with on their own time, in their own place, purchased with their own money, is really no-one else's business. When looking for reinforcers that are of the *play* type, you are looking for games or toys that they actually like rather than games or toys that they are supposed to like.

104

I ♡ to have ...

On my bathroom counter I have a little carving of an otter as he would look floating on his back in water. I don't know what the stone is but it's a beautiful green. Sometimes when I'm in the bathroom I just sit and touch my green otter. (*Don't even think it.*) I love it's feel (I said, **Don't go there**) and the sensation of joy it brings to me (OK, OK, I should have picked some different example).

Interestingly, no one who has ever gone in to my bathroom has ever commented on the otter. Now that may be because they are taken aback by *The Encyclopedia of Unusual Sex Practices* which I leave there for bathroom reading. It also may be because the otter means nothing to anyone but me. Whenever I see it I remember a trip to give a lecture in a beautiful town in northern British Columbia called Prince Rupert. The shop I bought it in was cluttered full of the neatest stuff. I am a browser by nature and I was in clutter heaven. Just on the way out I saw this little otter guy all by himself in a dusty bin. He came home with me and now resides happily by my sink.

Now tell me that you don't have items that are completely personal, absolutely important and essentially valueless to others? Ain't it great having things that are more than *things*? When looking at this category of reinforcer you just need to see the things that the person gives value to. These would be potential reinforcers.*

Yes, this is a footnote. I am doing this for the reviewer who said something like, "Hingsburger's work would have greater credibility if he made at least occasional use of footnotes." So here it is.

*please make sure to read the ethical concerns about the use of reinforcement when working with people with disabilities before utilizing any *to have* reinforcers.

You know that reviewer was right, I already feel more, I don't know, academic. I think I'm ready for Herring Bone Tweed and leather patches. This ends the footnote.

I ♡ to talk and be talked with

Some folks just love to talk. Some just love to listen. The first group, in one of nature's great errors, is much larger than the second. For some people social interaction is a huge reinforcer. The opportunity to spend time with others chatting is the reason people hold cocktail parties. When looking for social reinforcers you are looking to see what kind of social being the individual is. Do they love groups of people or do they like being alone? On a car ride do they prefer to look at the scenery or do they want to yak, yak, yak?

This is the group of reinforcers in which you would look at the individual's response to verbal reinforcement. Do they like it? Remember not everyone likes praise, some feel it manipulative, others get embarrassed, some are disbelieving. Think of your own reaction to praise. Isn't it dependant on who does it, how they do it, under what circumstances, and for what motive. It's complex, isn't it? I'll bet there are people who say of you, "You know <*your name here*> just hates to be complimented." And I'll bet there is a completely different group who say, "Wow, that <*your gender here*> just lights up when you say something nice about <*your best attribute here*>." So this means that you need to STOP and WATCH a variety of interactions, don't go on the viewpoint of just one person.

(As a complete aside, I'm curious, did you have no difficulty in the above paragraph filling in your name, your gender [at least I hope that was easy, if you have trouble with this there is a simple test, but that's another book] but had a heck of a time figuring out what attribute that someone would praise?" If so, you may need to work on some self concept stuff yourself. This is just an aside, not a footnote.)

I ♡ to touch and be touched

I remember being in a first year psychology course learning about reinforcers. In that course they broke the reinforcers down into different categories, the first being primary reinforcers. These were the cool reinforcers. Food and Sex being the two that I hit on right away. WOW the idea of Sex as a reinforcer may not be new, may not be ethically sound, but WOW. Last week I was teaching a five day class on how to teach sex education to people with disabilities. On the Thursday, different groups taught a short class on some sex education topics. One of the groups used an exercise wherein people had to comment on a part of their body that they particularly liked.

You should have heard them! *I like my eyes 'cause they're blue. I like my hands because I have slender fingers. I like my hair because it shines.* This is day four of a series of classes on sex and not one person, not one, mentioned their, you know, pee pee. So when they got to me. I said it flat out. I like my genitals. They asked why. You got that right. A group that is going to go out and teach sex education asked me why I liked my genitals. I leaned forward and said, "Because they are the only part of my body that doesn't mind getting up and going to work." That broke the tension, let me tell you.

Touch reinforcers include more than sex. (Which all women know and all men get tired of hearing about.) Hugging, kissing, hair combing, tickling, wrestling, playing patty cake, arm wrestling, are all forms of touch that people can find reinforcing.

 Warning! Warning!! Warning!! Please note, that it's imperative that you read the ethical section of this chapter.

Reinforcement is Natural

It's important again to state that reinforcement and the use of things like food as a reinforcer and motivator is something that occurs naturally and regularly in social interchange between people. Has anyone ever taken you out to dinner to thank you for doing something for them? Let's say you took care of your best friend's kids in an emergency, or say you offered to pick them up after work when their car was broken down. Let's then say they take you out for dinner.

Now you are out for dinner with your friend. Do you see this as a *salary*? Of course not, the idea of being paid to do something nice for another can be very offensive. Do you see it as *manipulative*? Of course not, you saw it as a means of them saying "Thanks." Did you *expect* it? No? Well think about it before you answer too quickly. While you may not have expected dinner out, what would have happened if the person didn't do or say anything to thank you? In the future would you have been more or less likely to do the same thing for them if they showed you no gratitude for having done it? My guess is, unless you are a chronic doormat, you would think "I'm being used, they never even say, Thanks!" So let's admit that at least on some level we expect our nice actions for another person to have some kind of reward attached to them.

We not only expect rewards, we'll work damn hard to get them. The other day a friend and I were driving through town and saw a guy with a "I work for food" sign hanging around his neck. My friend joked and said, "Heck, I work for sex." We laughed and then I realized that if people, for one day, hung signs around their necks saying what they work for we would end up with the list I have just gone through with you. Pick your sign...

> **I WORK FOR COFFEE CHEESE CAKE**

> **I WORK AS A MEANS TO KILN TIME.**

> **I WORK FOR TOYS. BIG TOYS. LOTS OF TOYS. I LOVE BEAMERS!!**

> **I WORK FOR A WORD OF PRAISE............ LIKE THAT'S REALISTIC**

So we all might as well admit it. Money is simply a token with which we can use to purchase things we want or things we need. It's odd that people get killed over paper covered in bad art and ugly ink! You can't eat it, sleep with it, wear it to work, park it in the garage or take it for a walk. Yet the love of money is the route of all upheaval.

110

Ethical Concerns Regarding the Use and Mis-Use of Reinforcers.

I have two concerns regarding the use of reinforcers when teaching someone. (Notice I said that I have a problem with the use of some reinforcers, I don't have a problem at all with reinforcement. These are very different things.)

Problem #1 Everything I have been writing about the use of reinforcement has been with the idea of *positive* reinforcement in mind. Reinforcement simply means to increase a behaviour. The word *positive* when used with the word *reinforcement* means adding something in. So translating the clinical concept of *positive reinforcement* for someone's behaviour into lay language one would simply state *after someone has performed a behaviour, giving them something extra with the goal of motivating them to do it again or to try harder*. It's a simple concept that sometimes gets misused.

Let's look at a common situation. A person with a disability is learning to talk calmly at the dinner table. The staff decide to use their dessert as a positive reinforcer for them successfully meeting the goal. Now here is your question. Based on what I've said, is the dessert a positive reinforcer? Well, no, it's not. The idea of a positive reinforcer is that someone gets something extra, an extra bit of praise, extra time to play with a toy, extra attention from a staff. What often happens is that people use *already*

111

occurring situations or *already owned stuff* as reinforcers. This is unethical.

When designing a program that looks at the use of reinforcement the teacher needs to see what the person finds reinforcing, then see what they are already getting and then ensure that whatever is used as a reinforcer it's *more than* the person gets now. So instead of using the dessert as a reinforcer, they would do what? Right, they could offer an extra scoop of dessert.

The same is true of other activities or things that might serve as a reinforcer. One agency actually designed a teaching / behaviour program that used family visits as a reinforcer. If the person didn't do something right the person would lose family visits. This is wildly unethical for a couple of reason's. The first being WHAT!! The second being it ain't positive reinforcement if it isn't more than what they are getting now. You could, of course, note that the family visits three times a month and tell them that when they work all the way through the day the family will make an extra special visit. THAT is positive reinforcement.

What if you noticed that someone had a favourite hat and you set up a program that involved you taking his hat when he arrived at work in the morning and that if he worked through the day he would get his hat back. What's wrong with this? Well first, it involves a thing called *theft*. (That pesky Criminal Code gets in the way all the time, eh?) Second, it isn't positive reinforcement because he already has it. Third, what would you do to someone who took something you liked away and said you could only have it back if you learned something new or did something their way? Right, me too. Could the hat be a reinforcer? Well, what if he was allowed to wear his hat for extra time during the workday if he did well?

Positive Reinforcement is great because it means enriching the life of another person. If it doesn't enrich, it isn't ethical. Period.

Problem #2 Be very careful about the use of physical reinforcement. Touch that involves a lot of body contact like hugs, or is intimate like kisses and hair stroking, or is childlike like sitting on the lap, is dangerous at any time. There are so many other potential reinforcers that it is probably best to leave the touch reinforcers out of it if it is anything past a high 5 or a pat on the shoulder.

If this makes you uncomfortable because you realize that if you aren't offering this kind of reinforcer then the person won't get touched, there is a problem. The problem is that they need someone appropriate in their lives to offer them physical contact. Let's get on to one of the friend making programmes or a dating skills program really really fast.

Using Reinforcement

The discussion of reinforcement strategies will be

done in much greater detail in the final of the behaviour books. What follows is a brief discussion of schedules of reinforcement as they pertain to teaching.

What do these three things have in common?

1:     "That's right"

2:     "Uh huh."

3:     "Good, Good, keep it up."

That's right they are small verbal reinforcers that encourage someone to keep trying. It's almost natural to use them constantly through an initial few teaching sessions. They are wonderfully generic being appropriate across age, gender and learning situations. It's also quite natural for the frequency of their usage to drop (but not disappear) as the skill of the learner increases. Without knowing it, most who teach use a variety of schedules of reinforcement. Their primary purpose of reinforcement is to keep the process going, scheduling reinforcement is to help maintain the skill once it's learned.

Schedules of reinforcement refer to how we schedule reinforcement. (I love writing sentences like that!) In order to understand this let's take a look at the schedule of reinforcement usually used at the beginning of a learning program:

Continuous Reinforcement: This is where you reinforce continuously. (Do you think you'll be able to pass this as an exam question?) At the beginning of a learning program the teacher usually uses a lot of reinforcement. The criteria for a learner to receive reinforcement is usually quite low and the teacher may be reinforcing any kind of co-operative behaviour that even approximates what the learner is attempting to do. If you are teaching vacuuming, for example, you wouldn't begin the program with an expectation that reinforcement wouldn't be given until the room is completely free of dust and debris. You would begin by reinforcing the person for just coming with you to the room and, if you were using backward chaining, turning the vacuum off when the room was clean. Throughout their attempts to hit the off button, and if you have my brand of vacuum cleaner this skill require a great degree of flexibility and dexterity, you would reinforce everything from pointing at the button to attempts to press it. The number of reinforcers would be greater than the number of times the machine is shut off, it would be equal to the number of movements and attempts that the person made that ended in the vacuum successfully turned off. This, folks, is *continuous reinforcement* and while it sounds like a lot of work, it really does happen quite naturally.

Clearly, it would not be advantageous to stay at continuous reinforcement. This form of reinforcement is really only used to get the person into the skill and then to motivate them to keep trying. As the person learns the skill the amount of reinforcement drops. Let's say that our learner has completed the vacuuming program. Now you are reinforcing the person at the end of every successful learning session where they vacuumed the entire room. What kind of reinforcement program is that? Right, it too is *continuous reinforcement* because you are reinforcing every successful trial. The difference between this example and the previous one is that the criteria have changed but the rate of delivery of reinforcement hasn't. It's still after every time the criteria are successfully met. But you aren't going to stay here are you. You will probably start reinforcing every second time the person has successfully finished vacuuming. We are now at a new style of reinforcement:

Fixed Ratio Reinforcement: This means that you will be reinforcing after a predetermined number of successful trials. Reinforcing after every second trial is a Fixed Ratio of 2, in shorthand FR_2. You might then go to FR_3 or FR_4 as the person begins to feel confident in themselves and require less and less reinforcement. If you are using a Fixed Ratio reinforcement program it probably means that you don't feel that the behaviour has established itself to the point that the structured reinforcement plan is no longer necessary. Once they have gone past this it is typical to then go to a different kind of reinforcement plan.

Variable Ratio Reinforcement: This means that you will be giving reinforcement at different times. This comes fairly close to the way that our behaviours are naturally reinforced. We aren't reinforced every time we do our hygiene, but occasionally someone will say, "Gee you smell good!" or "Gosh, you always dress so well!" or (if you grew up in my home) "You don't look like crap today." These occasional bits of reinforcement are enough to keep us at the task.

What you will have noticed by now is that this form of reinforcement is good for behaviours and skills that can be reinforced for performance. But there are a whole lot of things that need to be reinforced not for a performance but for the length of time (or interval) the person spends "at it." Let's say you are wanting to teach someone to stay at a task for a work period. At present they may be sitting down to work for only ten or twenty minutes and your goal is for them to work for an hour. How would you begin?

Continuous Reinforcement: Here we are back to that old standby. Starting at the beginning is important. By reinforcing constantly throughout the time they are working will motivate the learner to go past their already established endurance level. There are two problems with the use of Continuous Reinforcement when reinforcing time. First, to do it you would have to practically sit with the person for the whole time. This isn't practical given the fact that the agency probably has given you a few more responsibilities that need to be done at the same time. And you won't want to stay at this level very long. More probably you would begin with a ratio form of CR. We have already noticed that the person can work for ten to twenty minutes. By working at getting the person to a consistent performance of twenty minutes, you could use a Continuous Reinforcement

Schedule with the criteria being twenty minutes. Once there you can switch to an interval schedule of reinforcement.

Fixed Interval: All this means is that you predetermine what the interval will be, say every five minutes. *Variable Interval* could also be used and would involve you giving reinforcement on a more randomized schedule say, five minutes, then ten minutes, then seven minutes, then fifteen minute, then thirty minutes.

The most important thing to remember when using schedules to fade reinforcers is that fading to zero is a really big mistake. Reinforcers need to become natural and if possible internal. (This will be a major issue addressed in the next book.)

Chapter 8
Success Comes in Cans!!

Let's put all this together in a quick and easy way. It is difficult to teach well. Think back to your own teachers and I'm sure there are those who bring a smile and those whose mere memory gives you gas. Further, the number of teachers you had who were good people but lousy as educators is probably pretty high. So let's acknowledge that teaching is a skill. It requires more than simply good intentions. So here are the principles of good teaching...

(sorry, editor sorry ... you wanted the chapter called...)

22 Principles of Good Teaching

1. *Never let the learner fail.* Set it up through careful planning that the learner always ends a teaching session with a sense of success.

2. *Know how the learner learns.* Spend some time watching the learner interact with their environment. See how they learn in a variety of situations. Ask questions of those who know them well. Find out the best strategies to teach the learner.

3. *Become a reinforcer to the learner.* Establish a rapport with the learner. Make sure they know that you are a safe person to be with. Have some fun, share some laughs, develop mutual trust and respect before you

119

do anything else.

4. *Teach what makes sense.* Make sure that you are teaching something that will make a difference in the life of the learner. Ask yourself this question about your teaching goal, "When we're done, will this make a difference in the learner's life?" If the answer is, "No" or "Not really." Look for another goal.

5. *Respect the disability.* Make sure you understand how the learner's disability makes them a unique learner. Be careful not to excuse the learner from learning because of their disability or to hold the disability responsible because your teaching plan didn't work. You need to know now how the learner has already triumphed over their disability to learn the skills they already have. This will enable you to work with their strength to overcome a potential weakness.

6. *Respect the task.* Something that you've been doing for years can seem so simple. But remember that once you struggled to learn it too. Something as simple as tying shoes requires a complex set of skills. No task is simple while it is still unlearned.

7. *Know the task.* Spend time doing a task analysis so that you know each of the steps and can easily guide the learner from step to step. Be aware of the step size and be ready and willing to break each step down further if necessary.

8. *Be prepared to teach.* Make sure you have everything you need in easy reach. This may sound ho hum as a bit of teaching advice, but organization helps. Every time you interrupt the teaching process to go get something you mess up the transition from step to step and from practice to habit.

9. *Know the difference between teaching and recording.* Teach. Measure success. Two different jobs to be done at different times.

10. *Be ready and willing to reinforce.* Know what the learner likes and be ready to give a payoff for effort and for accomplishment. Be liberal in your interpretation of success and make sure that the learner knows that at the end of the struggle there is reward.

11. *Provide ongoing feedback.* Let the learner know how things are going throughout the task. There should be a sense that you are there to assist but not take over the process. Ongoing feedback that acknowledges both effort and accomplishment can keep the process from becoming frustrating.

12. *Work logically, building skill upon skill.* Forward chaining or backward chaining, it doesn't matter but work in a way that is systematic. Try to build one skill on another.

13. *Begin with the end in mind.* Remember to work towards

121

an end product. If this is a skill that is going to be used in a whole bunch of different environments, then teach in different places, at different times, in differing situations. This will allow the learner to practice skills in a wide variety of places at the very start. Trying to generalize a skill once it's been learned may be even more difficult than taking the time to teach generalization along the way.

14, *Do it over, repeat, try again.* Make sure that the learner has many opportunities to practice. Remember that repetition doesn't mean boring. Get creative and teach in a variety of different ways. But people with developmental disabilities by and large require more opportunities to try before they learn a skill than those without learning handicaps. So give them chances but keep them (and yourself) interested at the same time.

15. *Give the process time.* Remember it takes time to learn! So don't give up too quickly. Also don't try to push too much teaching into too little time. Go at an easy pace, you have time, use it.

16. *Motivate by building "learning esteem."* Make sure that there is lots of reinforcement for success but ensure that the learner comes to see themselves as *able* to learn. Remember that you are teaching them both the skill and the desire to try new things at the same time. The older the learner is the more they may

have come to expect failure, it's imperative they experience success.

17. *Evaluate constantly.* As learners begin new tasks they may experience a lot of frustration with the task, with themselves and with you. Be cautious and judicious in setting goals for individual teaching sessions. Too much and the learner may tire from the struggle to learn. If you sense growing boredom or frustration, change tactics or revert to a known skill, reinforce and end.

18. *Evaluate regularly.* Don't let years go by before asking, "Why isn't the learner, learning?" Every couple of months take a look at your data to see if learning is occurring. If not come up with a new strategy.

19. *Celebrate all achievements.* It is important to liberally use reinforcements throughout the teaching sessions. But when the learner achieves something really significant, stop and celebrate. Do something bigger. Have a "I learned it" celebration.

20. *Pat your own back every now and then.* You realize that you are teaching the "unteachables" don't you? Look in the mirror and say, "I work miracles every day of my life." Say it because it's true.

21. *Wait ...* Do you know the person? Have a relationship with them? Is there trust between you?

Have you looked closely at their life and ensured that you are teaching what they need rather than what you need?

22.   *Gain* ... a sense of perspective ... a sense of purpose ... a sense of priorities ... a sense of phun. These are the four senses of any good teacher.